THE GIMMICK
AND OTHER PLAYS

BY DAEL ORLANDERSMITH

**DRAMATISTS
PLAY SERVICE
INC.**

THE GIMMICK AND OTHER PLAYS
Copyright © 2003, Dael Orlandersmith

All Rights Reserved

CAUTION: Professionals and amateurs are hereby warned that performance of any or all of the Plays in the volume THE GIMMICK AND OTHER PLAYS is subject to payment of a royalty. The Plays are fully protected under the copyright laws of the United States of America, and of all countries covered by the International Copyright Union (including the Dominion of Canada and the rest of the British Commonwealth), and of all countries covered by the Pan-American Copyright Convention, the Universal Copyright Convention, the Berne Convention, and of all countries with which the United States has reciprocal copyright relations. All rights, including without limitation professional/amateur stage rights, motion picture, recitation, lecturing, public reading, radio broadcasting, television, video or sound recording, all other forms of mechanical, electronic and digital reproduction, transmission and distribution, such as CD, DVD, the Internet, private and file-sharing networks, information storage and retrieval systems, photocopying, and the rights of translation into foreign languages are strictly reserved. Particular emphasis is placed upon the matter of readings, permission for which must be secured from the Author's agent in writing.

The English language stock and amateur stage performance rights in the United States, its territories, possessions and Canada for the Plays in the volume THE GIMMICK AND OTHER PLAYS are controlled exclusively by DRAMATISTS PLAY SERVICE, INC., 440 Park Avenue South, New York, NY 10016. No professional or nonprofessional performance of any or all of the Plays may be given without obtaining in advance the written permission of DRAMATISTS PLAY SERVICE, INC., and paying the requisite fee.

Inquiries concerning all other rights should be addressed to The Gersh Agency, 41 Madison Avenue, 33rd Floor, New York, NY 10010. Attn: Seth Glewen.

SPECIAL NOTE
Anyone receiving permission to produce any or all of the Plays in the volume THE GIMMICK AND OTHER PLAYS is required to give credit to the Author as sole and exclusive Author of the Play(s) on the title page of all programs distributed in connection with performances of the Play(s) and in all instances in which the title(s) of the Play(s) appears for purposes of advertising, publicizing or otherwise exploiting the Play(s) and/or a production thereof. The name of the Author must appear on a separate line, in which no other name appears, immediately beneath the title(s) and in size of type equal to 50% of the size of the largest, most prominent letter used for the title(s) of the Play(s). No person, firm or entity may receive credit larger or more prominent than that accorded the Author. The following acknowledgments must appear on the title page in all programs distributed in connection with performances of the Play(s):

THE GIMMICK
Created and originally directed by Peter Askin.

The Gimmick was originally produced by McCarter Theatre in Princeton, New Jersey.
Emily Mann, Artistic Director; Jeffrey Woodward, Managing Director.

The Gimmick was presented at Long Wharf Theatre, October 27 – December 6, 1998.
Douglas Hughes, Artistic Director; Michael Ross, Executive Director.

Originally produced in New York by New York Theatre Workshop.

MY RED HAND, MY BLACK HAND
My Red Hand, My Black Hand was commissioned and given its
world premiere presentation by Long Wharf Theatre.

BEAUTY'S DAUGHTER
Beauty's Daughter had its New York premiere at the American Place Theatre,
January 25 – February 26, 1995.
Wynn Handman, Artistic Director.

MONSTER
Originally produced in New York by New York Theatre Workshop in 1996.

SPECIAL NOTE ON SONGS AND RECORDINGS
For performances of copyrighted songs, arrangements or recordings mentioned in these Plays, the permission of the copyright owner(s) must be obtained. Other songs, arrangements or recordings may be substituted provided permission from the copyright owner(s) of such songs, arrangements or recordings is obtained; or songs, arrangements or recordings in the public domain may be substituted.

*I'd like to dedicate this book to my brother, Osceola Fletcher,
my aunt Marion Thomas,
Peter Askin, alchemist/director/great friend,
and to the memory of my mother, Beula Brown,
who makes me wrestle my demons.*

CONTENTS

THE GIMMICK 7
MY RED HAND, MY BLACK HAND 37
BEAUTY'S DAUGHTER 55
MONSTER 91

THE GIMMICK

THE GIMMICK was originally produced by the McCarter Theatre (Emily Mann, Aristic Director; Jeffrey Woodward, Managing Director) in Princeton, New Jersey, on February 26, 1998. It was performed by Dael Orlandersmith and directed and conceived by Peter Askin.

It was subsequently presented by the Long Wharf Theatre (Douglas Hughes, Artistic Director; Michael Ross, Executive Director) on October 27, 1998. It was performed by Dael Orlandersmith

It was first produced in New York by the New York Theatre Workshop on April 16, 1999. It was directed by Chris Coleman.

This play was developed in part with the support of the Sundance Theatre.

THE GIMMICK

The voice of Ms. Innis is heard in darkness.

MS. INNIS. Dear Alexis, Mt. Morris Park / bright and sunny today but there is always darkness underneath / Some people survive the darkness / learn from it / face the darkness and conquer it / others do not / I'm sorry to say / your friend Jimmy was found dead among leaves and waste / My hope — my prayer — is that this news will bring you peace. / I'm looking at Mt. Morris Park again as I write this / there is darkness but behind it there is beauty / there is light / Paris, they say, is beautiful this time of year / maybe I'll visit you there one day/ hope to hear from you soon / proudly / Ms. Innis.
ALEXIS. It's 1968 and everybody / they're listening to Archie Bell and the Drells "Tighten Up" and as they dance, shout their shouts of "Ah, Get it, work out!" and I got a toy / a click clack and the Black Panthers and the young lords them / they scream "pick up the gun" / I look up at my house and I see my mother's cigarette smoke / inside curling, curling toward the ceiling / only women in the living room / no men / only women passing a bottle between them / menless / some are sad about it / being menless / others glad / all I see is my mother's cigarette smoke / she's sitting by the window looks out at me waves / her eyes glassy / not out of focus yet / soon they will be / eyelid movements will be slow / not yet.

I continue to play with my click clack / two hard balls hitting together, "Watch it, them things can hurt you if they fly off that string" / Tootsie says to me as she passes and curses / and young boys and young girls come around the block / "she's fat and doofy" / they point and say "doofy, you doofy" / and I yell "your mama is" / they stop "what I know you didn't say nothing bad about my mama / I'll jack you up / mess you up / jack you up" and I say "let's go."

But this boy / he smiles to me / smiles to me not laughed at me / paint in his hair / some of the paint / it had gold flecks and landed on his eyelashes / his eyes were golden / golden eyed black boy smiling to me / "I'm Jimmy / I'm ten years old / I paint I used to live on 145th and Lenox that's real real real west Harlem / now I live here / we / me and my pops / live here in east Harlem / that's where we are now / how you doing?" and I smile back / at the boy / Jimmy / "I'm Alexis / I heard about you / they didn't tell me / the kids 'cause I don't stick with them / I heard them talking about you / how you paint" / and he smiles at me / and smiles some more and Archie Bell and the Drells sang "now make it mellow."

And somebody / a man walking down the street with a rakish hat / a drunk man attempting a pimp walk / walking behind two girls / staggering / staggering / stumble man was trying to pimp his walk / wanted the player to be in his walk / he / the man / looked at the girls' asses slurring "shake that moneymaker" me / I'm laughing / laughing real hard / playing with the click clack / on my stoop / me and Jimmy are on my stoop / watching the drunk man / the stumble man / on the sidewalk / my mother drunk in the window / upstairs in the window with the curling cigarette smoke / with the menless women complaining / and down here this drunken man / trying to pimp "I like young girls / shake that moneymaker" / drunken man with a rakish hat / trying to walk the walk / walk a pimp / cool / tough walk / and I say "that man is stupid / a stupid man" / Jimmy's eyes fall / fall to the ground / he chokes / sounds like he's choking / "that's my pops."

We go quiet / real quiet / except for the street sounds and somewhere the music changes to Marvin Gaye and Tammi Terrell / it's real quiet / strange how quiet it was / or maybe it seemed quiet / Jimmy more quiet than me.

I hear laughter from my window / my mother still there curling cigarette smoke / thick / thick / her eyes now out of focus / doesn't see me / I point to her "she's my mother" and Jimmy looks for a second / looks at my mother she's got a cigarette and a filled glass in the same hand / Jimmy nods / and says "grown people, man" and I say "yeah / parents."

Later Jimmy calls from the streets / he's carrying paper / paper filled with paint and gold / rolled up drawings / taller than he is /

huge huge drawings taller than Jimmy / pictures with paint and gold / "Alexis, Alexis" / never rings the bell / "Alexis, Alexis" his eyes big real big / his eyes said "let me come up / please be my friend, please" / his eyes said / he didn't say it with words / his eyes said.

I open the door and let him in / my mother's there / I say "this is Jimmy, Jimmy's my friend" / Jimmy's eyes go to her face / down to the ground to her face down to the ground "he's not good enough" her eyes say / "will grow up to be no good" her eyes say as she looks at the boy / with colors tangled in his hair and raggedy shoes / she knows all this my mother does by looking at the boy's shoes / by standing above him / looking down at his raggedy shoes and Jimmy knows how she feels but doesn't have the words / her eyes don't meet his eyes / he knew / felt / saw / she didn't think he was good enough.

He mumbles "your mom don't like me Alexis / she don't like me" / "yeah she does" / "no she don't / she don't like me / "she don't know you yet / I don't know you good but I like you / give it time" and me and Jimmy go to my room and he shows me pictures he's painted / lots of pictures / all over the room / there are pictures of Superman / Superman with captions / DRUGS CAN KILL / Superman living in Mt. Morris Park killing drug dealers / pictures of Superman being friends with a small black boy / SUPERMAN'S BEST FRIEND JIMMY / "He talks to me, Superman does" / "Jimmy, I will fight all crime / I will let no one hurt you / you're my friend / you and all children" / "I tell people he talks to me / they say I'm lying, but I don't care / he talks to me in a secret language / nobody else can understand / I paint Superman 'cause he's good / see how he can fly Alexis / he can fly / nobody can touch him / he can fly."

"What do you like to play, huh Alexis? / What do you like to do?" / I show him a notebook with a story / I'm scared but I give it to him / my notebook "you can read it" I say / outside I say "you can read it / inside I say "don't laugh at me" / outside I say "I'm going to be a famous writer one day" / inside I say "don't laugh at me don't tell the other kids on the block" / outside I say "I write a lot even though I'm eight years old. I like to write I'm not like these stupid kids around here" / inside I say "the other kids don't like me. They laugh at me. Be my friend you read my story and be my friend."

He looks at my notebook / frowns / looks and frowns / shakes his head / inside I say he's laughing at me, laughing at me, I'll beat his ass / jack him up for laughing at me / outside I say "gimme it back / you don't like it / gimme it back" and I snatch my book "no no Alexis I ain't good with words" / "I don't understand" / "me neither" / but he didn't laugh at me / he was my friend / he didn't laugh / and I read the story to him.

I read about a girl / a fat girl who lives in a dirty house / then wakes up thin in a clean house / and Jimmy says "that girl, that's you right? / Alexis / that girl is you right / I can tell that's you" / but I say "it's my friend it's not me. I know someone it's not me" / Jimmy looks long / hard / deep / "no not no friend it's you Alexis / it's you."

Later we go to Jimmy's house / his house a motherless house / we're watching "American Bandstand" and boys and girls on beaches and Jimmy and me, we're watching / we're watching on TV / "American Bandstand." Girls and boys dancing on top of cars and behind those cars / in the background is blue water / pure blue / blue water — so pure and we, Jimmy and I, don't notice that their hair is long and different colors than ours. How their hair sways / ours didn't / their eyes — blue / green / ours brown / maybe we know but we didn't know. We were seven and nine or maybe eight and ten and "we're going to leave Harlem when we grow up" / "leave Harlem / leave the ghetto." / Gonna grow up and dance on the beach / on top of cars with blue / pure / water / That "we were going to the clean / blue / blue ocean / gonna dance near the ocean on top of old cars." We're watching "American Bandstand" / It's Saturday and it's "American Bandstand" and we're watching the beach / the kids on the beach / "Look Alexis. See the water, it's so clean" "I see it Jimmy. Yeah it's real clean. That's where we're gonna live / We're gonna live on the ocean" / Jimmy he screams "We'll eat fish right out the ocean / and I'll paint pictures of the ocean" / fish right out the ocean.

Jimmy's father steps in front of the television / He's blocking our view of the ocean / Can't see the ocean / He turns the TV off / "Y'all watching dat whitey shit. That got nothin to do wichy'all. Watching that cracker shit. You can't live like them." Jimmy's father looks through him "You stupid lil nigga talkin about how you goin somewhere an you can't even read. Can't even spell ocean

/ How you gonna find it?" / He grabs Jimmy by the arm / squeezes / squeezes his arm tight / brings Jimmy to his knees / Clarence looks at me "hey cute thing / what do you say / oh God you look so cute" Clarence winks at me / I look ahead / Jimmy's hurt / angry / but determined to be cool / maintain his cool.

Says "gonna get his money, Alexis / gonna get it / watch and see" / he turns to Clarence / Jimmy stands eyes fixed on Clarence / if looks could kill / but remains cool / Jimmy's cool / turns to Clarence "Father, would you like me to go to the store? / your gin is low" / Clarence lets go of his arm / mumbles / fumbles / fumbles some more / digs in his pocket / pulls out a twenty / "yeah, yeah, nigga, go to Sam's, get me my gin."

We're outside / "is this a twenty Alexis?" / Jimmy laughs / Jimmy cries / with gold on his skin / a shining / shining boy / "is this a twenty Alexis?" / I say "yeah Jimmy it is" / Jimmy smiles a triumphant smile / "my father / so drunk / gave me a twenty / gin only costs three dollars and fifty cents / I don't care what my father says we're gonna live like the kids on TV, Alexis."

Jimmy and me didn't know / didn't see black or white / we were kids / we saw / but we didn't see / We didn't understand why we couldn't live like "American Bandstand" kids on TV / me and Jimmy we prick our fingers / mix blood and say / I love you love me / forever and ever / you and me.

My mother Lenny / Lenore was actually her name / sat by the window in Harlem, smoking / by the window / waiting for her boyfriend who long since stopped coming / still my mother sat smoking and waiting / sometimes when I talked to her she didn't hear me / she's looking out the window / smoking and waiting / didn't hear me / she was dreaming / dreaming / maybe of being young and pretty again / young and thin / she said she was thin when she was young / she said "thin and pretty / thin and pretty / to be thin means to be pretty" / she shakes her head as if saying "why can't you be thin and pretty?"

Lenny moves from the window / not dreaming now / makes me stand on a scale / my flesh measured by numbers / if my flesh weighed less I was good / could do better / my flesh if it were heavier made me bad / evil / "how could you do this / gain weight" she said / "disgusting," my mother Lenny said / her flesh hanging loosely over her pelvis / "disgusting," she says / slapping my buttocks / pulling my arms / I'm eight or nine or nine or eleven / I'm on the scale / my flesh measured by numbers / "disgusting," she says / her words were worse than the sting of her belt / her words / my mother Lenny's words left invisible welts / scars / her words / when I close my eyes / made me think of Orange Red Black Blue / I wanted soft words / kind words / words that when I close my eyes made me think of caresses and kisses.

"Dear Diaree: God made me big and fatter than other kids and it makes me feel bad when people call me fatty and I cry sometimes I wonder where people go when they die if they go into the clouds. Heaven is up in the sky and once when I was in a place and we went through a cloud I thought I was gonna see my grandmother but I didn't and I was sad 'cause I never saw her before and I wanted to say hello so I don't know where dead people go but I know they leave here and maybe they go through clouds and disappear and sometimes I want to disappear too OK I have to go now bye diary yours Alexis. Oh, ps. I love to read and in school they gave us the Bobbsey twins and I like it a lot all the pictures and stuff of them in the books I love and their neighborhood looks clean I wish I had a clean neighborhood to play in OK now I do have to go see you later Alexis."

It's summer and Mr. Softie ice cream cone truck is on our block / we heard it before we saw it / Mr. Softie truck / Jimmy runs / tears down the block / "Alexis / come outside / come on ice cream man is here / he's here / Mr. Softie ice cream cone truck is here / see him / I'm treating / you don't have money / I'll treat you / you're my friend / I'll treat you" / I run out / meet Jimmy / we're taking long licks / long wet licks / of our soft cones.

"Know what I heard, Alexis? / Tootsie's a hoe / yup wearing short dresses / kissin on men / she ain't nothin but a hoe / what's a hoe, Alexis? / you know? / I hear it all the time / hoe this / hoe that / man what's a hoe / my pops said, "boy, women ain't nothin but hoes" / is that true Alexis? / when you grow up are you gonna be one? / is your mother one?" / I lick my soft cone, "a hoe is a lady who does it for money / I ain't lettin no man kissin on me / nasty / I ain't doin no nasty with no man / my moms ain't no hoe" and Jimmy licks / shakes his head "my pops says all women are hoes / but maybe you ain't gonna be a hoe / but I still say / if all women are hoes / when you grow up / how can you not be one? / but I guess that you don't let nobody touch you / if you don't scheme out wit nobody, you can't be no hoe / make sure you don't scheme out and let some man feel you up / you'll be a hoe then / if some man tries to make you a hoe don't worry, I'll kill him / you're my friend / you're not dirty Alexis / you're not dirty / you're my friend."

Other kids are gathered around / they're buying cones too / licking sweetness / youthful sweetness / we're excited by this / licking our ice cream cones we could have been kids anywhere / we were like kids anywhere / the sweetness meant good / the sweetness meant underneath we wanted goodness / we licked our cones / excited by the sweetness which felt good going down our throats / melting in our stomachs / the goodness melted in our stomachs / we wanted goodness to melt in us / we the kids in Harlem / like all kids / any place / jumping toward the ice cream man / screaming toward the ice cream man / we're reaching for goodness / we're reaching for the sweetness of childhood / the sweetness meant no Gimmicks / no Hustle / we the kids in Harlem / were sweet / it was there / it is there / the hope / the sweetness / There was / is a Beauty in Harlem / Beyond Gimmicks and Hustles / Next to Gimmicks / Hustles / there is a Beauty / back then me and Jimmy had hope.

Later, we're older. Wise to the Gimmick but me and Jimmy didn't wanna pick it up like Sukie / this girl in our block / who steals a car / She's "gonna leave Harlem" she says / "riding a car" / a stolen car / "wanna leave it all behind" she says / in a stolen car. Me and Jimmy knew it / the Gimmick / but didn't want it / Not like Sukie / not like Tootsie / or anybody who went down with Tootsie / in Tootsie's house / Jimmy's father had Tootsie / Everybody's father had Tootsie / her house was full of Hustle 'n' Gimmicks / Hustle 'n' Gimmicks / anybody who had the silver / the people White Black Yellow Brown / all Tootsie cared about was anybody who had the silver "Nigger Whitey Spic Chink I don't care" she said / Tootsie was always talkin about men / dope / money / Her house was the low place / filled with men / dope / money / anyway she could get it / and sometimes her Gimmick / she tried to make it soft / make herself delicate / tried to Gimmick being a "Lady" *(Imitates her.)* "I can't stand here wichy'all. I got to go and get dressed 'cause John is coming. Gotta look good for

John." And we laugh at Tootsie / 'cause all men to her are named John / like Jimmy's father / anybody's father / it was hard for Jimmy to take. For Jimmy knowing his father was with Tootsie / "Why" / "Why'd he have to go to her / my father / Why my father" he said / why anybody's father / Tootsie has five men named John / those five men got wives 'n' kids / and me I laugh and Jimmy half-laughs and says "Oh John's comin? Which one / Tootsie?" / She bends over / throws up her gown and says "Kiss my ass / kiss it / y'all can kiss my ass / with Tootsie it all boiled down to ass" / cash / money / dope / the total Gimmick / *(Beat.)* How could anybody stand that? How could Jimmy stand it?

We were always old, still we got older and more guarded / I mean you had to / you became more guarded in the neighborhood / with family that don't / can't understand 'cause they can't take anymore in / 'cause with them it's / Do you have some Gimmicks / you drug it / you drink it / Do you have some more / they can't won't take anything in / can't see it / not clearly 'cause it was / is can you drug it / drink it / can you snort it / can I drug / drink some more / can I fuck it / drug it / drink it? Do you have a set of Gimmicks I can shoot this with? And the Gimmick is also / looking at the cracks in your wall you call home / realizing it's a ghetto / your home is a ghetto / wanting to leave it but not having the courage / the Gimmick is not reinventing yourself / thinking someone owes you something / the Gimmick is being down, so low, low to the Ground not knowing / realizing you have a choice / or maybe you do realize you have a choice / and you care and leave / or don't care at all and stay / don't care

and you shoot it

cut it

stomp it

scream it

The Gimmick is blood / a blood circus / how much blood can pour onto the streets of Harlem / on our block in Harlem / there's the Gimmick / there's the Gimmick / gonna live by it / die by it / the Gimmick / back then we knew we wanted more.

I grasped books / hungered to read / which is how I found the library / I knew that the library was filled with books about the Bobbsey Twins / There were words / words and more words / It was quiet / no fights / loud music / quiet / still / and I read here / I write here / none of the kids on the block come here / "it's corny" / they say / they see me going in / or going out "fat doofis goin to the library / fat doofis" / I yell "mind your fucking business."

(Beat.) The lady that works there / stares at me / she stares at me / outside I say "hello" / go through books / listen to certain records / write in my diary. Inside I say "why is she looking at me? What did I do wrong? / Did I do something wrong?"

The lady just stares / stares / I turn my back / focus on books / the books are worn / some have pages missing / I don't care / I take the books / the pages / sometimes I smell the pages / like inhaling words.

I'm aware how the light hits the books / How the dust rises with the light / the sunlight specifically hitting the books that very few people here read / I want to read all these books / I get upset when I see that they're torn / why can't the books have all the pages / I think when I grow up I'm gonna have a house filled with books / every room will be filled with words.

My mother says I should get out more / "be more with the kids," she says / they don't like me / the kids just want to play all the time / I like to play but not all the time / I like quiet / quiet and books / when I read books / words / I close my eyes and let the words help me get to places / with words / I close my eyes / I don't see Mt. Morris Park / or a set of used, broken Gimmicks / I close my eyes / I see towers, endless landscapes / when I open them / when I open my eyes / words disappear / I see the ghetto / where I live / smell the stench of where I am.

Later I want other things to read / I want to read about people like me / I go to the lady that's always staring / I lie: "I have to write a paper about somebody from Harlem that became famous" / "you come in a lot / I've seen you for a long time reading / writing in your journal" / outside / I say "yeah" / Inside I say "you think I'm a joke? / Don't laugh at me / I'm not a joke."

The lady / the librarian says / "Books are good / words are tools / people who write books put ideas on paper and let us know we're not alone" / outside I say "oh good" Inside I say "why is she telling me this? / what does she want?"

The lady librarian brings a book / she sits next to me at a table

/ "this man came from the streets of Harlem / he used words to carry him off the streets of Harlem and yet take aspects of Harlem with him / his words / his use of words are universal / what's your name?" / "Alexis" / "Alexis you like books / love books / this is good / very good / use words, Alexis / let those words help form ideas / this writer I speak of / this man / this great man from Harlem did that / James Baldwin / his name is James Baldwin" / she looks towards Mt. Morris Park / towards noise.

There's a man and a woman / "motherfucker I need twenty dollars / I'm sick / I need my wake-up shot / I need to get off" / the woman's crying / moving side to side shaking / her need to Gimmick is strong / her nose / running / her nose is running / the man tries to block her blows / "I don't have twenty dollars / what's wrong witchoo / I ain't got it / I'm sick too / I need my wake-up shot too / I don't have / twenty dollars."

The librarian shakes her head "'People who don't invent themselves / who are so bitter / so blinded / who cease to question / have made peace with defeat' / he said that / Don't waste yourself / Don't / read / use words / go to libraries / see other places like Baldwin / Don't waste yourself" / She lends me James Baldwin / the book *Another Country* / "somebody may say 'this is too grown-up / why are you giving this to a child / she's barely a teenager' / but what's in here / you've seen / you've heard / you're a Harlem child / a child of Harlem / you know / use the words, Alexis / use them / drink them / don't waste them don't waste yourself / you're too young to leave Harlem but for now, see places beyond Harlem in books / see things Alexis, don't waste."

Outside I say "what's your name?" / her eyes return to Mt. Morris Park / "Ms. Innis" / outside I say "I gotta go now Ms. Innis / see you later" / I get up and leave with James Baldwin / outside I play cool / nod and say, "that was cool." Inside I say, "thank you."

I read Baldwin / James / Jimmy Baldwin / That night I call Jimmy / "Man we gotta / start to hang outside of Harlem / we gotta go to other kinds of movies not just Bruce Lee flicks / ever read Jimmy Baldwin / his name is Jimmy / just like you / there are more libraries / better libraries than on 124th St. / Man Jimmy we gotta take the subway downtown / it's only a subway ride downtown / we can get there / no time for Gimmicks man / the world's big / let's take the subway downtown."

A Harlem Black boy and a Harlem Black girl and "California Dreamin's got nothin to do with us" / Me and Jimmy are 10 and 12 or maybe 11 and 13, we're walking / walking downtown / walking together / we always walked on Saturdays / "downtown Saturday" where the beat of the street changes / there's sound but not noise / We do this / can do this / not just on "downtown Saturday" / Monday. Wednesdays any school days / or days we want / when some teacher / who doesn't get what we're saying / can't hear / feel what we're saying / you got classroom / me and Jimmy got the streets — "Let's meet on 96th Street and Madison Avenue Alexis" and I say "Okay, Jimmy" and we're on the streets / on the streets / a group of downtown kids say to each other — "Let's go to the museum," / Jimmy and me we look at each other — "Let's go Alexis / wanna go? / Let's go / never been to no museum before / let's go."

We go / the Modern / we go / drink Picasso / He grabs my hand / "That's me Alexis / that's how I feel / damn, that's it / that's it / if I could only paint like this Alexis. I probably can't" / I say "You will Jimmy you will."

Later we're in a bookstore / I fondle / caress books /
"My mother taught me purple
Although she never wore it
Wash gray was her circle
The tenement her orbit
My mother reached for beauty
And for its lack she died
My mother taught me purple
She could not teach me pride"

"I'm gonna do this Jimmy. Gonna be a word magician. And you're gonna paint, paint great art / Gonna make great art / They're not gonna touch us."

For many days we sat on Harlem stoops exchanging / trading dreams he'd say "okay Alexis you go first" / "I'm gonna be a famous writer. I'm gonna go to Paris / find James Baldwin and tell him I'm from Harlem too. / Now you" "I want to be a famous painter like Picasso" I say "Jimmy you're gonna be better than Picasso" and Jimmy and I, we're no longer on a Harlem stoop / we are on the

Champs-Elysées / the Left Bank and we are drinking coffee / on the Left Bank / we sit in cafes at night with Picasso, Baldwin, we're drinking espresso, smoking / we're smoking Gauloise, drinking wine 'n' cognac / we dine on cheese and bread / Harlem's long gone / long gone / Hustlers and Gimmicks finally put to rest. With knees clasped to our chins we huddled on the stoop together / swearing / when we grow up we could do it / you and me / we can do it us / you / me / together / gonna put this ghetto thing down / gonna turn our back on this ghetto thing.

If I could unlock all the doors / break all the locks / break down doors and locks / I'd come out / but I hear voices / and the voices / the voices are hard / I retreat again

I write this / show it to Ms. Innis / sitting at our table in the library / Ms. Innis sits with her back to Mt. Morris Park / her eyes on me / she smiles / "I like it Alexis / you keep writing / I think you should" / I play cool / outside playing cool / inside I say "is she just playing with me? She's full of shit. Does she mean it? She's full of shit. She better not be playing with me / I'll hit her / I don't care how old she is" / outside I say "can I bring you things I've been doing / writing poems and stuff?" / I look out at Mt. Morris Park / playing cool / trying to play cool / waiting for her answer / scared of her answer / need a yes / want a yes from her / Ms. Innis reaches for my hand / "Alexis, I'd be honored" / her hand is warm on my hand / I love her / wish she were my mother / I want to tell her I love her so bad / outside I answer "cool."

I spend time in the library writing / reading / dreaming / Ms. Innis sneaking me sandwiches and hot tea / "you're not supposed to eat here, it's our secret," she says / her body, Ms. Innis' body, was big, strong, graceful / nails always clipped / she smelled of perfume / scents she collected from places I read about in books / "you're a strong, healthy girl Alexis / You don't know it yet / I hope you find it / for yourself / you're something special" / I say nothing / I drink my tea / eat the sandwich that she made for me / Ms. Innis called me "special" / inside I feel warm / even pretty for a minute / but I have to go home soon / I say "I have to leave soon / not now / but soon" / I continue to drink my tea / I eat my sandwich.

The next week Jimmy brings me to his teacher's studio / Mr. Kaufman's studio / He smiles a slow smile, talks in a cool voice / a voice trying to be cool because he's really excited / "I have the key / Mr. Kaufman gave me the key / says I can paint here whenever I want / Mr. K, he's a brother / he's a brother / and know what else he said Alexis? / He said 'Jimmy / you have something special to give the world / so special' / I want to be / I want to be so bad Alexis / so bad / if I could be great Alexis" / he stops / looks around at Mr. Kaufman's studio / then in a whisper / more like a whisper / says "God Alexis / God / maybe there is one / a God / huh, Alexis? / maybe there is one / I feel so good, man" / he spins and grins / spins grins / stops / "maybe I can't Alexis / maybe I don't deserve to do good" / and I say "naw man, hush, hush / cut that / cut that / Jimmy" / "Damn Alexis" he lights a joint / I say "Naw naw Jimmy you don't need it / it's good with Mr. Kaufman / you don't need to do that / no, you're great, trust me, heart to heart."

Jimmy paints / paints angry pieces / frightened black boys / frightened black girls / crying black boys / crying black girls / Harlem's Munch / there's one piece / one / a black boy / a black boy in a chair with colors / colors of Orange, Red, Black 'n' Blue / this boy sits in a chair by a kitchen window in Harlem / looking through locked bars onto an empty street / the boy's eyes are wide / sad / "know what I call that piece / I call it Solo / that's the name of it, man / Solo."

It was the color spectrum of pain / pain in total color / slashes of light / color / Jimmy knew it from Clarence / I knew it from Lenny / How each slap / punch / was a spectrum of orange red black blue.

One day I say to Jimmy "Let's make the colors happy colors / not just hurt colors / let's make them happy" / Jimmy frowns / frowns some more "What do you mean, Alexis" / I say "Not just orange-red blood, Jimmy / Think of something good with orange-red" / Jimmy says "I can only think of blood, Alexis" / "But blood keeps you alive, Jimmy / Think about it keeping you alive / Like when we go to Paris / blood keeps you alive" / Jimmy grins / grins some more / "Red-orange blood is life / not just pain / it's life" / And I say "Yeah, Jimmy / life."

I'd watch him and he'd paint me / I'd let him paint me / he'd paint me heavy boned / heavy eyelidded like Picasso's women / he'd paint my hands, large expressive / my shoulders sloping big fine boned / He'd see the browns and yellows of my shoulders and I say

"You should paint my breast too Jimmy" / His eyes get big / "Yeah okay / you sure" / "Yeah, I'm sure" / I remove my shirt / it was strange / in Jimmy's room / it was still / quiet / still and strange.

Then it got fine / real fine / "You're doing it Jimmy just like Picasso. / We're gonna go Jimmy. We're gonna go to Paris. We'll meet twice a week / you paint me / I'll write / we'll go / When we're eighteen we'll go."

Now Jimmy really begins to paint me / before it was pencils / crayons / sketches / now he is totally on canvas / painting me on canvas like Picasso's women / heavy boned / heavy eyelidded / Jimmy glows "this is for you Alexis / do you like it / man I hope you like it / couldn't have done it without you / you my muse / you my muse Alexis girl" / glowing / glowing / he gives me my portrait / a swirl of colors / not just Orange Red Black and Blue / my portrait was gold / I saw gold / I was gold / "now everybody can see it, Alexis / How beautiful you are" / Jimmy made me look / strong / beautiful / Perhaps Jimmy saw those things because those things were in him / strength / beauty / but he didn't know it / He didn't know he was filled with so many colors / not just hurt ones / many ones. / We set a time twice a week / I'd sit before him naked. "Big is more better. Notice how Picasso makes his girls Big Alexis?" And I'd write and read my words in Broad strokes / He broad stroked with paint / I with language / I'd create color with language / And the world was endless / Endless strokes of paint / Endless words on paper / How endless the world was.

"Alexis, man Mr. Kaufman / that dude / he's money / guess what? / I showed my paintings / drawings of you / he loved it Alexis loved it" / I get angry "that's between you and me Jimmy / That man / he saw me naked? / that's between you and me / why'd you do that" / Jimmy says "no, no, no, Alexis just like Picasso's women / remember? / not about sex / you know that / like Picasso's work / know what else he said? / he said 'that this work can take you far Jimmy' / and he showed my work to a friend of his who's got a gallery downtown / you believe that shit Alexis? / and the man wants to show my work in his gallery / you believe it?"

We go see Clarence in his bar The Silver Rail / wearing another rakish hat / Clarence / still trying to pimp / still trying to talk to "young girls" / "whachoo want, man whachoo doing in here" / Jimmy's excited / jumping / almost dancing / Jimmy's almost dancing says, "Pop, check this out / a teacher, my teacher in school / he likes my artwork / and he showed it to a friend of his / and his friend owns a gallery / and his friend wants to show my work / my work / Pops / that's cool, right" / Clarence / mumbles in his gin / drinks deeply of his gin / looks me up and down / "grow'n up, huh Alexis / gettin you a fine frame / fine frame / somebody gonna get to it soon" he says / eyeing a woman in a short skirt / "Did you hear me pops / pops, did you hear me?" Jimmy said / Clarence is still looking at the girl in the short skirt / the short short skirt.

"How much money you makin / you makin money wit dat drawin? / them whiteys payin you?" / Jimmy stops dancing / "I don't know / I mean / I didn't ask / Mr. Kaufman's my friend / I trust him" / Clarence fans his hand away / "boy — cut dat drawin shit out, man / don't come in my bar wit dat bullshit / whynchoo shoot some hoops, man / don't come in he'ah / comin in my bar wit dat" / Clarence turns to the girl in the short skirt / "shake dat money-maker" using old-timey slang "shake that money-maker" old-timey slang / Jimmy's head goes / down / down / "let's leave Alexis" / I say "don't worry Jimmy. He'll be sorry after you get famous / you'll see / fuck him."

It's amazing / what parents can do / how they can beat you and say it's all right / I gave birth to you / I can beat you / I feed you / I can beat you / I clothe you / I can beat you / I can talk to you any way I want / I brought you in this world / I can talk to you any way I want / I'm trying to teach you / I'll knock your head off / If I have to / I can talk to you anyway I want / you're not grown / you don't pay bills here / I can talk to you anyway I want / try and leave / you don't like it / try and leave / I'll talk to you anyway I want / wanna scream child abuse / go ahead / I don't care / I gave birth to you / I'll talk to you anyway I want / I go first / you're nothin / I'm the parent / I go first / compared to me you're nothing / wanna scream child abuse? / go ahead / who do you think you are / you think you're gonna rule me / do you hear me talking to you / you're nothin / I'm the parent / you're the child / I brought you here / in this world / I gave birth to you / I pay the bills / I go first / I can talk to you anyway I want / *(Beat.)* Parents — they're a real Gimmick.

We go downtown to the gallery / we're walking / running towards it / "Come on, Alexis, gotta surprise for you girl / you'll dig this / you're gonna be surprised" / I see me / nudes of me on the wall / Jimmy's nudes of me on the wall / it was me / and it was Jimmy / Jimmy stares / squeezing my hand / "That's my work up there Alexis / that's me up there / see it? / that's you up there / you're my best friend and muse. God that's me on that wall / I'm not famous like Picasso yet / not yet / maybe I will one day be huh, Alexis?" / He swirls / whirls / dances / jumps / "I'm an artist Alexis / I'm fifteen years old and I'm a real artist / I'm on the wall with other artists / I'm in a gallery / a for real gallery."

The next week is the show / the official show / the official opening / "Oh God, Alexis / I got no clothes man / I got no good clothes / I got to be clean for this opening / we both do / do you have clothes? / cool clothes? / we gonna deck out for this, Alexis / we gonna be totally decked out, Alexis / I'll buy you a new dress / need a new dress / I'll buy you one / we'll go in a taxi too, Alexis / we'll go in a taxi / we'll come back in a taxi / decked out Alexis, girl / we gonna be decked out!" / we go to antique stores in the East Village / I find it hard to find pretty things in my size in department stores / they're ugly / polyester/ old lady clothes / we go to the East Village 'cause / "we want to look like real artists / 'cause we are real artists / no disco people" / I said "we gonna look cool / way cool / not like disco people / we're gonna be great."

Jimmy gets a forties suit / baggy jacket and pants / black / "I got a white shirt to wear with this / silk / no tie / don't need no tie" / we find an aviator scarf / a long black scarf / Jimmy wraps it around his neck and grabs a beret / "I got it Alexis / I'm gonna wear this / this is how I'm gonna look!"

We go to the women's section / I'm still having a hard time finding things in size sixteen / the dresses are still old lady dresses / polyester and sickly yellow / I'm getting depressed / more depressed / I'm feeling fat / ugly / fatter / uglier / "Jimmy there's nothing for me here / nothing / I'm glad we got something for you / but there's nothing here for me / I'm mad / I'm getting madder" / Jimmy says "don't worry, Alexis / Mr. K's daughter / Genevieve / her name is Genevieve / she works in Fiorucci's / you know the clothing store? / maybe she can help / let's go."

We hop another train / get off at 59th Street / go into Fiorucci's / there is throbbing disco music / small / skinny girls with blue / pink / orange hair / some of the clothing is interesting / nothing in my size / Jimmy is talking to a girl / a white girl / a white girl dressed in white and beige / a skinny white girl / I get cold / for a minute / I get cold.

"Hi I'm Genevieve / Jimmy says you need something to wear / how about a long shirt with a vest / we can do that / there are no dresses in your size / but there's some nice shirts that are long / they cover the hips and you can wear a cool vest Annie Hall type vest" / and before I can answer Jimmy yells "yeah, yeah / I'll buy it / yeah Alexis."

Genevieve goes to get the shirt and vest / Jimmy yells again / "she's cool / doesn't she look cool Alexis / she looks like something out of Modigliani / doesn't she look great?" / I look at Genevieve / the white Modigliani girl / the white Modigliani girl dressed in cool white and beige / I get cold for a moment / I feel fat / ugly next to her.

(Beat.) She comes over smiling and hands me the long shirt / "see, it's nice / covers the hips / here's the vest" / it's a long white shirt / tailored man's shirt and vest / it covers my hips / I roll up the sleeves / it looks okay / it looks okay / I say "it looks okay / thanks" / she / Genevieve / doesn't try to sell me bad clothes to look bad / she doesn't / doesn't have to / the clothes are fine / she / Genevieve knows the world likes thin skinny girls / skinny / thin / white Modigliani girls / the world does not like big / black / girls at all / not at all.

Opening night / Jimmy's downtown / leaves without me / calls, "Sorry, Alexis, had to get there early." / I say "cool" / I put on my spandex / shirt / beret / neighborhood people stare / some mumble "weird" / "looks like a butch" / I don't care / I'm a full full Picasso woman / I'm walking Harlem streets feeling strong and cool / strong and cool / off the subway to the gallery / half-running / half-walking / I get there strong and cool.

I get to the gallery / first paintings I see / Genevieve / Jimmy's portraits of Genevieve / Genevieve's orange / red paints / not hurt oranges / not hurt reds / bold / her colors were bold / her hair flying / lips parted / kittenish / silent sighs / lips meant to kiss /

Genevieve's got lips boys want to kiss / she's got lips they get lost in / Jimmy / does Jimmy want to get lost / get lost / her thin lips / his full lips / lost in Genevieve / in her kisses / go to Paris / cool breeze walk / with Genevieve / in Paris.

I go through the gallery / all the people / white people in the gallery / they smile / tight smiles / men / women / rich rich / they seem rich / they surround Jimmy / smiling / they surround him / some of their hair sways / like on TV / long straight / swaying hair / like on TV / holding drinks close to them / talking close together

I think he's interesting
I don't see Picasso at all
The wine is very good
Who's this Jimmy again
I think he's talented
Are he and Genevieve going together
Jimmy, are you really from Harlem
He has an interesting way of using color — I do see the Picasso influence
I don't understand
Music is playing / Stravinsky they taught us in school / Stravinsky / *Rite of Spring* / then Parker / Charlie Parker / they the white people / bop to Parker / cigarettes and drinks / some in the same hand / other hands separate / other have hands that dangle cigarettes / looking at paintings / drinking / smoking / I spot Jimmy.

He's got a cigarette and wine-glass in the same hand / he never heard of / he's never heard of this wine / I walk up to them / Genevieve / she's holding her glass / she knows wine / she holds her glass / knowing wine / I feel awkward / she gives me kisses / one on each cheek / "like in Paris" / he says / Jimmy does the same / mimicking a Paris kiss / "gonna find out about this Paris kiss, hunh? hunh, Alexis?"

Mr. Kaufman / he takes pictures of them / people surround them / taking pictures of them / they hug each other / pictures of them hugging each other / crowd moves in more / I'm pushed out / Jimmy / he looks at me / not saying what his eyes are saying / His eyes say "it's not my fault, it's not my fault" / looks at me / yells / "stay Alexis, stay!"

I go outside / my legs no longer mine / try to hail a cab / none stop / some slow down / see I'm black / drive on / others don't acknowledge me at all / I'm invisible / I'm black / invisible / I'm anxious to leave / I want to go back to Harlem / I want to go back to my house / decrepit / violent / I don't belong down here / finally, I get in a cab / one stops / I get in the cab, no longer wanting to be a Picasso girl / I get uptown / I get inside the house / "I don't belong here either / with Jimmy I thought I belonged" / I take off the blouse / sit in a chair in the dark / for hours / watching the sun over Mt. Morris Park go from orange to purple to black.

For months / days / nights become the same / I'm watching people's lips move but I can't hear their voices.

I can see them together / he and Genevieve I see them / in my mind / I see them together / I wanna slice them / cut deep / wanna see blood / spill / spread / my Gimmick is strong / I'm walking / then walking faster / I still walk downtown / walking / downtown / walking solo / feeling bad / feeling so low / wanting to fight / it's no longer downtown Saturdays / It's solo / solitary Saturdays / no Jimmy / I go to movies / museums / libraries / I go alone / Jimmy's always in the foreground.

I see a girl / see / a rich white girl / I'm walking downtown / she's walking uptown / Jimmy's in the foreground / as always I see him / in the foreground / she looks at me smiles / smiles at me / I stop / knowing she's smiling at me / I stop / block her / not touching her / don't have to / I'm bigger / taller / I block her and say "what you laughing at / what're you lookin at? I'll fuck you up bitch" / the girl / the white girl / turns to walk past / I block her / she turns to walk past / I block her again / she says "why what did I do to you / I wasn't laughing at you / I smiled and said hello / what's wrong with you? / what are you doing / I said 'hi' / that's all" / outside I say "fuck you bitch / you think I'm funny" / inside I say "what am I doing?" / the girl / the girl who's white says "why? / why do you want to hurt me?" / outside I say "get out of my face / punk bitch / fuck you / punk white bitch" / inside I say "my God what am I doing / she seems nice" / I let her pass / continue walking downtown / solo / and Jimmy's always in the foreground.

There's a day I call Jimmy / I can't stand it / not talking to him / "Alexis, man / I'm moving up in the world / wish me well / I can't bullshit around / Genevieve is doing stuff for me / wish me well"

/ I say "she's using you / white girl, man / that's what it is / she's rich / white / and using you / she comes up here to Harlem / then goes back downtown / up here for kicks / downtown to live / I'm telling you / listen / you've got to / Jimmy / listen to me" / he cuts me off / yelling / he's never done that / yell at me before "you jealous, Alexis / jealous / you've never talked color before / what's with that / that racist shit / we were never into that shit / I'm going places / you jealous / I gotta go" / I scream back / "I was not prejudiced / not before / I was not / now I am / I hate white girls / I never was / I do now / I hate that bitch / I hate you too / you're nothin / you're a nigger / Jimmy / A no-good fucking punk nigger / I hate you / I hate that filthy white bitch too" / Jimmy yells back "fuck you / jealous ugly bitch / fuck you / I hate you."

I wish I were invisible / I despise nice days / nice days bring kids out onto the streets / I go to school / come home / do homework / housework / do some of what my mother tells me / I'm hard / I'm soft / I curse God / always I curse God / there is no God / he's never been in my corner / I hate Jimmy / I love Jimmy / can't we go back / why can't we go back / I hear the teacher's voices / they don't make sense / outside I go "yeah, yeah, okay right" / everybody is "yeah, yeah, okay alright" / Inside I say "I want to die / I hate living / I want to die" / food has no taste / I dress not prettily / clothing to hide in / words mean nothing / books just reflect / don't change / it's not real / I can't take words in / don't care to take words in / in my journal I write disappear / disappear / I can hear no one / nothing / I can't watch people / can't watch people hold hands / kiss / families / boyfriends and girlfriends / love / there is no love / no such thing / it doesn't exist / no one cares / I don't care / who cares.

Ms. Innis comes to my house / what is she doing here / she can't see me like this / I don't want her to see me like this / I can't look her in the face / don't want to look her in the face / "Alexis. I haven't seen you in months. Why don't you come to the library?" / She hears Lenny's slurred voice / I close my eyes / want to disappear / Lenny yells / slurry / slurry / "who is it?" / comes to the door / vodka glass filled / cigarette in the same hand / I close my eyes / I want to disappear / Ms. Innis' voice gets soft / "I'm Ms. Innis from the library / I'd like to speak with Alexis."

Lenny's eyes are out of focus / she tries to become Mother / Maternal / tries to talk proper / tries not to be slurry / "Let her in, honey" / Lenny, she calls me honey / slurringly calls me honey / "Alexis, honey, take her to the living room / take her. Pleased to meet you" / she's Gimmicking the proper lady / trying to be a proper lady / she, Lenny, was in the company of a proper lady / Ms. Innis / Ms. Innis was a true lady / she, Lenny, knew it / tried to emulate it / she, Lenny, couldn't touch it.

I close my eyes for a second and I let Ms. Innis in / she sees the house / inside I say "God, let me disappear" / the furniture / the smell in here / outside I play like I don't care / "I've been busy Ms. Innis / I haven't had time / in fact, I'm not into the book thing anymore / Ms. Innis closes her eyes / "words / books / words Alexis, are important / don't give up on them / I will not let you give up on them / do you hear me? / use words / use them / your friend Jimmy / I've seen him / I know he hurt you Alexis / deeply / I know how deeply you feel this hurt / Alexis, you need to feel it / then use it / put it into words / like James Baldwin / I will not let you waste it / you will not / we have the Russian writers to read next / you and I / one in particular / Tolstoy / who said 'art is not a handicraft. It is a transmission of feeling experienced by the artist' / you are an artist Alexis / you are ashamed for me to see how you live / your mother / your mother Alexis / I've known mothers like yours / trust me / books are the answer Alexis / you are an artist / you don't believe it yet, but you are / words / I will force words down your throat."

Ms. Innis gets up / her eyes locked on mine / "I'll see you tomorrow? / we'll discuss Tolstoy / there's also an Austrian writer we'll talk about named Kafka / we'll see each other tomorrow / Agreed? / We are seeing each other tomorrow." / outside I say "yeah, yeah Ms. Innis, yeah I'll be there" Inside I chant "Jimmy, Jimmy, Jimmy" / Inside I say "disappear / disappear / I just want to disappear."

Jimmy comes to the house one day / strange him coming to the house / colorless / no color around him / not shining / no glow / I watch his shadow / can't believe he's come / I can't move / for a second I just watch his shadow / I go to the door / I don't open it / I go to the door / he smiles / nervous / frightened / I think of when we first met / I think of when he came to the house for the first time as a child / a small boy child / I don't open the door / through glass / through the glass of the door he says "Alexis how you doin?" / sees I'm hurt / I think he sees / I want him to / I'm so glad to see him / I won't tell him / I'm confused / I won't tell him / I say cold / low / "What do you want? / I'm surprised you're not with Genevieve / she cut you loose? / I hope she cut you loose."

His head jerks down to his shoes, then to my eyes / "Alexis, I'm sorry / I'm so sorry / I got caught up / It came so quick / in my face so quick / I thought I made it / I did / I did make it / I was looking way beyond Harlem / Paris was right there / I could touch it Alexis / I could touch Paris / Mr. K / Genevieve / I felt like somebody" / they made me feel like somebody" / I'm still cold / not as cold and low as before but still cold / he sags into the glass as if reaching for me / he wants me to touch back / I want to but don't / through glass he says "Alexis I'm sorry, so sorry / please / tell me we're cool / we can be cool again" / outside I say "I don't know man, it's not that simple" / inside I say "I want to so bad" / Jimmy looks at me through glass.

He leans / seems to sag further into the glass / and a hush voice — not quite a whisper / "listen Alexis, I'm sorry I have to ask you this / don't hate me / but the portrait I painted of you / I need it / I know I gave it to you / if there's a way I'll get it back, but I need it / I can't explain why / please don't hate me / I swear / I'll paint you again / but for now I need the portrait."

I go / I get it / my portrait / Jimmy gave me a piece of myself / now he's taking it away / myself / he's taking it away / but I gave it to him / I had to give him the portrait / I half-open the door / "Here it is man, take it, sell it, I don't care" / remembering / dreaming on the stoop / remembering Mr. Softie ice cream / I'm not sure what I am / how I feel / Jimmy takes it / smiling at the portrait.

Later that night I see Jimmy go into Tootsie's house / glides to Tootsie's place / "my God Jimmy. Not there," I think, "Not there." That was the last place / can't get any lower there / that's the house of Gimmicks / the cop spot / the shooting gallery and we said we didn't want to go there / "What are you doing there Jimmy" I screamed / "What the fuck are you doing down there" / Not down to all her Gimmicks / men 'n' dope / anything for money Gimmick / men and dope / buy this / steal that / people nodding

/ scratchin / cokin / drinkin / chokin / and somebody's babies / Motherless / Fatherless babies / some naked / some dirty / and Tootsie a hard woman / hardrock woman / Shank and Shoot woman / a throw down woman / and the people that hang in her place / Dark men / Dark women / Don't care / 'Got nothin to lose people' / but Jimmy's got everything to lose.

I've got everything to lose and I go down / down to Tootsie's I see Jimmy's eyes / glassy / shiny / skin dull / colorless / no coloring / about to be Black 'n' Blue skinned / somebody's liquor in his hand / just like his father / "Don't do it Jimmy. Like your father does / with your cup filled / Slurry like your father, Jimmy. We're going to Paris c'mon Jimmy / We're goin, you and me / you and me to Paris."

"Yo, shut up" / somewhere I recognize a voice / I think / I say "Fuck you." / As he scratches and nods / scratches and nods / skin dull / colorless / about to be Black 'n' Blue / Jimmy says, "Why you do that / Why you wanna do that / he's awright / he's cool" And I can't believe he's defending a Darkman / Gangster man over me.

I get up I leave / On my way out Tootsie offers me Stuff 'n' Gimmicks / Stuff 'n' Gimmicks "You come again, Baby / You can make money too / you can make money / you young / they like 'em young / the mens / come back anytime."

I go out / walk for hours / we were gonna put the Gimmicks behind us / Gonna throw everything away / You wanna test me, so how far I'll go? / For you / wanna see how far I'll go? / I'd give up my love for language / words / I'd give up my love for language / words / I'd kill the colors in me / my words / emotions / thoughts / they'd no longer be words just / mumbles 'n' grunts / mumbles 'n' grunts / in Tootsie's you're narrowed to mumbles 'n' grunts / the color of my skin will be Black 'n' Blue / Black 'n' Blue / red, orange, Black 'n' Blue — colors that hurt / I'll do it too / Go down / down / For you / If that what it takes to get to Paris / If you don't believe me / I'll show you Jimmy / I'll Gimmick for / with you / I'll scratch and sniff / Give myself to Darkmen for you / I'll do it / I'll go down for you / How low, Jimmy? / How low will I go? / Bottomless / all the way / down / down to the ground.

Tootsie got stuff for me / She got it / stuff for me / I do it / I throw up / I scratch / I nod. Darkman comes over / Got me up against the wall / Clarence got me up against the wall / Darkman Clarence / rips off my panties / I can't move / the Gimmick is strong / I can't move / Darkman Clarence does the in & out / in & out I can't move / Doin the "in & out," "in & out."

Jimmy comes out of a nod / sees Clarence / "Pop what you doin / Oh God Pop / don't" / Clarence on top of me / reaches in his pocket / throws Jimmy a bag of dope / Jimmy breaks his nod / breaks his nod / grabs the bag of dope / doesn't reach for me / he reaches for the dope / "I'm sorry Alexis / Oh God Alexis / I'm sorry" / Jimmy didn't care about my colors / my hurt colors / my orange / red / black / blue / Jimmy couldn't move.

(Beat.) I leave / Go home / There's not enough soap / and water / I'm in the shower for three hours / there's not enough soap 'n' water / There's blood / Blood / Blood Lost my Cherry Blood / Blood for Jimmy / is this what men 'n' women really do / men and women really want to do.

Somebody's got to know / Somebody's got to know / it hurts / my mother / she'll know / my mother she'll take care of it / I'll tell her / tell my mother what happened / She blinks pours a drink / Blinks pours a drink.

(Beat.) She takes me to church / you're supposed to be pure there / no vodka / no scratch 'n' nod / we have no business in here. *(Beat.)* My mother / She cries there / "my baby" she says looking over at me "my baby" / Her tears are vodka tears / vodka tears / we're in a new house now / new House of Gimmicks / God's House / God he's a Gimmick / He didn't stop the Darkman / He didn't stop Jimmy from the scratch 'n' sniff / from the Gimmick / I look at Him / God on the cross / "He suffered for our sins" it says / He doesn't know about my suffering / Jimmy's suffering / Did nothing for me / God did nothing for me / He did nothing for Jimmy / Didn't keep Jimmy from the scratch 'n' nod / He, God, didn't save Jimmy from the Gimmick. He's a Gimmick / God is a Gimmick just like everything — body else / a Gimmick / a House of Gimmicks / I get up leave His house / Wanna burn His house down / burn His house to the Ground.

I'm in my room / I hear / Lenny as she vodka snores / she wastes herself on vodka / Jimmy he wastes himself on opiate dreams / makes me wanna waste myself / "Want me to waste myself, Jimmy?" / I say aloud in my room / he's not there / God / God / there is no God / I'm in my room cutting up clothes / clothes I had on when Clarence took me / bloody clothes / I cut up bloody clothes / ripping them with my teeth / with the scissors.

I bring them to my neck / want to slice myself / waste myself / slice myself / I close my eyes / Jimmy's in the foreground / scissors / I trace my neck face with the scissors / the kill yourself / kill myself voices / they're in my head / loud / clear / kill yourself / kill myself voices / I can hear them loud / Jimmy's in the foreground / in my head with the voices / gonna waste himself / gonna waste myself / erase myself / I look into the mirror / I see flesh / fat burdensome flesh / I see waste / waste / I trace the scissors over my body / it's waste / I want to end it / life / life's a Gimmick / the voices are loud / strong / somewhere I hear Lenny's voice / "why can't you be thin / pretty / thin / pretty" / the kill yourself / kill myself voices / all the voices / they separate / collide / separate / collide / Jimmy's in the foreground / I can see him nodding / nodding / opiate mumble nods / I trace the scissors / over my body / it's waste / I want to end it / life's a Gimmick / the voices are loud / I see the empty space / the space where my portrait was / where myself was / I gave him myself in the portrait / he took it / now I'm looking at the wall where it was / the space / empty.

The voices grow louder / there is no God / I'm still holding on to the scissors / want to slash myself with the scissors / Lenny she said Jimmy's nothing / I got dropped by a nothing / I'm nothing too / waste / waste / I'm waste / the scissors / I aim for my gut / trace my gut with the scissors.

I spot Jimmy / Jimmy Baldwin / I see his book / his words near the pile of clothes / how'd that book get near the clothes / I pick up the book / Ms. Innis / her words inside the book, to me / "Alexis, use words / do not waste / this man, Mr. Baldwin, knows the importance of words" / Ms. Innis writes a quote of his next to hers / "People who don't invent themselves / who are so bitter / so blinded / who cease to question / have made peace with defeat" / I hold the book like a friend / maybe like a lover / I hold caress the book / Jimmy's in the foreground / I can see him / I close my eyes / I can see him / I close my eyes / I can see him / the kill myself kill yourself voices are there / Lenny's thin and pretty voice there / I can hear those voices / see Jimmy in the foreground / I can see Jimmy / I can hear the voice / Ms. Innis somewhere / somewhere says "Don't waste" / and the other Jimmy / Jimmy Baldwin smiling / smiling to me / big grin / laughing eyes / smiling to me / he's smiling to me.

Ms. Innis / James Baldwin are louder than Lenny's voice / louder than the kill yourself kill myself voices / "words / use words" / I reach for my pen / I reach for language / for the words in me / those words will make me beautiful strong / will make Jimmy beautiful strong / will create beauty / my words / my stroke of words / I will make them / from Harlem I will make them carry me from Harlem to Paris / from ghettos to palaces / my words / my vision / and Jimmy's in the background / I'm in the foreground / I'm in the foreground / Paris on my fingertips / glittering on my fingertips. *(We hear the voice of Ms. Innis.)*
MS. INNIS.
Mt. Morris Park / bright and sunny today but there is always darkness underneath /
ALEXIS.
but I know the beat of Harlem / remember the beat of Harlem /
Because I have walked this walk before where razor cut glances can slice the skin of the toughest whore
MS. INNIS.
(V.O.) Your friend Jimmy was found dead among leaves and waste
ALEXIS.
I've heard this rap before
like when you get your first kiss and your first kiss is gonna bring music
and the music is going to swell and get bigger and bigger like in Italian movies
MS. INNIS.
(V.O.) My hope — my prayer — is that this news will bring you peace.
ALEXIS.
I've witnessed this scene before
like when somebody's mother chain-smokes while they drink
and they talk about when they were young
'cause when they were young men dug them
and they take a final pull on the drink

the smoke comes out their nostrils
they end the whole rap by saying "My God, ain't life a bitch"
MS. INNIS.
(V.O.) I'm looking at Mt. Morris Park again as I write this / there is darkness but behind it there is beauty / there is light.
ALEXIS.
I dreamt this somewhere before
I touched the shoes of Mary Magdalene on Avenue D
blood was flowing from her feet
Spanish dancers were hanging tough outside a shiny aluminum storefront
gutted tenements echo another dark black nigger future
phantasmagoria they call it
MS. INNIS.
(V.O.) I'm sorry about Jimmy Alexis / but you can hold onto him through your language /
through your words.
ALEXIS.
Somebody's popping chewing gum or maybe it's the click of a hooker's shoes pacing the
pavement at three o'clock in the morning
MS. INNIS.
(V.O.) Paris, they say, is beautiful this time of year.
ALEXIS.
Lovers are tongue-kissing in their doorways and the souls of young boys and girls are
trapped underneath the hoods of stolen cars
and love is something cranked up real loud on the dilapidated stereo for everybody in the
streets to hear
MS. INNIS.
(V.O.) Maybe I'll visit you there one day.
ALEXIS.
or maybe love is a rumble
or maybe it's Neptune putting on black velvet gloves
and simply dancing again

End of Play

MY RED HAND,
MY BLACK HAND

MY RED HAND, MY BLACK HAND was commissioned and given its world premiere by the Long Wharf Theatre (Douglas Hughes, Artistic Director; Michael Ross, Executive Director) in New Haven, Connecticut, on October 10, 2001. It was directed by Sarah Peterson. The cast was as follows:

DAUGHTER .... Mary Hodges
FATHER .... Jack Burning
MOTHER .... Sandra Mills Scott

MY RED HAND, MY BLACK HAND

DAUGHTER.
    My hands / red / black
    Dance to Rhythms
    Different / Various / similar rhythms
    My Red Hand it dances to the
    Rhythm of my Father's Blood / His
    Blood Beat / His red
    Man beat
    PURE RED MAN
    My father / his mother /
FATHER.
    Tlingit from Alaska /
DAUGHTER.
    Died giving birth to him
    She died /
    But she still whispered to him /
    My father / his father
FATHER.
    Santee Lakota
DAUGHTER.
    My father half Tlingit
    Half Lakota dreamer
FATHER.
    Transported
    Transported
    to Boston
DAUGHTER.
    He / my Father crying for his

Father / Drumming up the
Rhythm of his Father Through
Pent-up Angers
Wearing Eagle Feathers
FATHER.
Sign of the Eagle
DAUGHTER.
Sign of Scorpio — Nov. 4 / His birthday
My Father /
FATHER.
Eagle Born
DAUGHTER.
Scorpion
beat his
hands to the rhythm of
his Father's Ghost
His Father / My Grandfather
FATHER.
Spent
Depleted
American Dreams / Stomped into the
Dirt of the Res /
DAUGHTER.
His American
Dream /
FATHER.
to pick up
a Guitar
To be a Blues Man
To be a Red Man / Blues Man —
DAUGHTER.
My Father's Father / My Grandfather
FATHER.
Ghost danced Lakota Style
DAUGHTER.
to
his father / my Great-Grandfather's rhythm
but he closed his eyes and also

Ghost dances with
FATHER.
   Robert Johnson /
   Mississippi John Hurt
   Blind Lemon Jefferson
DAUGHTER.
   He / my Grandfather couldn't leave it /
FATHER.
   The Res —
DAUGHTER.
   They wouldn't let him leave it /
   The Res /
FATHER.
   — you're not True to
   your own
DAUGHTER.
   — they said
FATHER.
   "you're not proud to
   be a red man"
DAUGHTER.
   they said —
FATHER.
   "If you leave / Don't come
   back /
DAUGHTER.
   Don't come back
   to the Res — they say
   He / my Grandfather Looked
   into my Father's Eagle eyes
   A Child's eyes / knowing
   eyes / an old child's eyes /
   His eyes — my Grandfather's eyes
   Said
FATHER.
   Take the world / make
   it yours / Rock the world
   You can Rock

DAUGHTER.
   Rock
FATHER.
   Rock
FATHER and DAUGHTER.
   Rock the World
DAUGHTER.
   My Father Glides Eagle-eyed from the
   Res and the Tlingit island /
FATHER.
   Leather-Jacketed / Eagle-
   eyed /
DAUGHTER.
   Blues and Tlingit / Lakota riffs
   dripping from his fingers /
FATHER.
   Chuck Berry /
DAUGHTER.
   Tlingit riffs
   dripping from his fingers /
   Leather-Jacketed and Guitar ready
   Just like Chuck Berry or
FATHER.
   Link Wray
DAUGHTER.
   — Link Wray
FATHER.
   — a Shawnee
   from North Carolina
DAUGHTER.
   — A RED / Blues
   Rock 'n' Roll man /
FATHER.
   — a cool man
DAUGHTER.
   My Father cool — Just like Link Wray
FATHER.
   Slick

DAUGHTER.
> — Just like Link Wray
> Ghost dances Lakota Style / Tlingit Style
> and Rock 'n' Rolled / a Steady
> Rock 'n' Roll bop
> and Somebody on the Res says
> "How could you do that / Leave /
> us / How could you? /
> You're not proud of your own
> kind" / Somebody on the Res says /
> they say "wanna be a white
> boy? / Wait till they call you a FeatherHead" / Someone
> on the Res says
> My Father stares straight ahead

FATHER.
> Eagle-eyed /

DAUGHTER.
> proud and
> Eagle-eyed
> Outside

FATHER.
> — Standing tall

DAUGHTER.
> Inside — Rumbling
> The voices of the Res rumbled /
> inside of him but he continued to
> dance /

FATHER.
> Ghost dance /

DAUGHTER.
> The Res voices Got Louder /
> He continued to Blues dance /
> Blues / Red / Blues / John Lee
> Hooker dance / he had to
> take the voices and shoot them
> down / Vodka
> Tequila
> Bourbon

Hide himself in a woman's
Skirt / to kill the voices
Vodka
Tequila
Bourbon
Another woman's skirt / gonna shoot
it right
Down!
My Black Hand —
My Mother's hand / A Black Girl
Girl from Virginia / my mother /
MOTHER.
   a
Sharecropper Black Girl from Virginia /
DAUGHTER.
Her mother / my Grandmother
MOTHER.
   Lynched /
   it is Hard Time Virginia /
DAUGHTER.
   no
Different from Hard Time Mississippi
MOTHER.
   "Don't walk anywhere
   except in Darktown"
DAUGHTER.
   they told my
   mother
MOTHER.
   "Just stay in Darktown"
DAUGHTER.
   — they told
   my mother
MOTHER.
   "Darktown" was where the
   Dark people lived
DAUGHTER.
   they

weren't Black Then
They were colored then
and where they lived was
"Darktown"
My Mother / Sharecropper Black Girl / Big Black Girl
Knew about Trees
MOTHER.
Knew about the Bodies that hung from
those trees
DAUGHTER.
and the people who wore billowing white sheets
My mother's bare feet
MOTHER.
were blistered
from Tar and Dirt Roads /
DAUGHTER.
Those feet Shifted themselves
MOTHER.
into high heels /
DAUGHTER.
She wanted to Chuck Berry Bop
in her high heels /
She wanted
MOTHER.
to "Sport high-heeled shoes"
DAUGHTER.
She wanted
MOTHER.
her hair slicked back
pressed and curled /
DAUGHTER.
She wanted
MOTHER.
to Lip Balm
her lips — "Ruby Red" Just Like
The Ray Charles Song /
DAUGHTER.
She wanted

MOTHER.
> to snap her fingers /
> Slick-headed and curly sporting
> high-heeled Shoes to the
> rhythm of cities /

DAUGHTER.
> She wanted to Enter a
> New Rhythm
> Explore

MOTHER.
> — not just the
> Rhythm of Southern men
> Clinging to Mojo /

MOTHER and DAUGHTER.
> She wanted a city

DAUGHTER.
> She leaves Darktown
> Slick / curly-headed
> high heels and fingers snapping and
> clicking /
> She goes to Boston —
> sporting high-heeled shoes
> There are Dances /

FATHER and MOTHER.
> yes

DAUGHTER.
> There are Dances
> People will always Dance
> My Father sees her /
> He sees her at a dance /
> His Eagle eyes / connect to
> her Brown / Black Girl Eyes

FATHER.
> Eagle-eyed RED man /
> Mother
> red-lipped high-heeled Black Girl

DAUGHTER.
> The Hucklebuck Dance

meets
The Ghost Dance
And the Colored People / Before
They were Black / The
Colored people said
MOTHER.
— "Whachoo doin
with him / Some Red Man /
What do you want with him /
Some Red Man / That FeatherHead
dancer / whachoo doin
with him"
DAUGHTER.
And the Skins on the Res
said
FATHER.
— "You didn't get
an Indian Girl / one of our
Girls / Got a Dark /
Darker / NIGGER Girl / not
a Girl from the Res /
What are you doing with her /
Why didn't you Get a Girl
From the Res! /
Come back to the Res!" /
DAUGHTER.
They — my Father
my Mother
They both hear the voices /
FATHER.
Voices from the Res /
DAUGHTER.
The Tlingit Voice that whispers in his ear
MOTHER.
Voices from the Virginia Fields
DAUGHTER.
They — both — my Mother and Father
try to Ghost Dance / Blues Dance

47

    Drink away the
    Voices
FATHER.
    — Western / Northern Red voices /
MOTHER.
    Southern Black voices
DAUGHTER.
    They dance
    Snap their fingers
    Guitar Lick / try to
    Shoot it on Down
FATHER.
    Vodka
MOTHER.
    Tequila
DAUGHTER.
    Bourbon
    They try to shoot the voices down /
FATHER.
    Boom
DAUGHTER.
    Boom
MOTHER.
    Boom
DAUGHTER.
    Boom /
    Shoot them all Down —
    A year later — they marry —
    A year after that
    I crash through amniotic Fluid
    and blood /
    I crash but
    silently my mother says
MOTHER.
    — "She's so quiet" /
DAUGHTER.
    my Mother says

FATHER.
  — "Makes no noise"
DAUGHTER.
  my Father says
  I hear his voice but rarely him/ he usually
  Speaks through guitar fingers / his fingers speak on his guitar I see him /
  long-haired / this man / red man who just spoke / my father — this red man
  this big red man / beautiful man
  I am a part of him
  My Father
  I hear him
  But
  I can't speak
  But I can hear
  I can't explain / I'm a baby
  But I feel it
  I feel them
  Turning on themselves
  Turning on each other
  not always with words
  There's looks
MOTHER.
  shrugs
FATHER.
  silence
MOTHER and FATHER.
  more silence /
DAUGHTER.
  I feel it /
  I feel them
  Shooting Themselves
  Down —
FATHER.
  Boom
MOTHER.
  Boom

FATHER.
　Boom
MOTHER.
　Boom
DAUGHTER.
　Later I'm a child /
　not a baby / a child
　I see it / smell it
FATHER.
　Vodka
MOTHER.
　Tequila
DAUGHTER.
　Bourbon
　I hear it my Mother's
　Black Southern voice slurry / shot down voice
MOTHER.
　"I love
　him / He's my husband /
　my man / I'm
　NEVER Gonna Leave / I love him!"
DAUGHTER.
　The Black Southern / voices / the
　voices are now Black from
　the Virginia fields / The 1960s
　and the voices are now Black
　tell her / my Mother
MOTHER.
　— "your child
　is a Nigger / FeatherHead / a Nigger FeatherHead" —
DAUGHTER.
　My Mother / she Vodka
MOTHER.
　Tequila
DAUGHTER.
　Bourbon
MOTHER and DAUGHTER.
　Cries

DAUGHTER.
    I hear it in my
    Father's voice — more so
    in his fingers / Fingers
    sliding up and down his guitar
    Vodka
    Tequila
    Bourbon crying
FATHER.
    Lakota / Tlingit guitar / Blues a shot Down
    Red
    Blues
    Bruised
    Man
DAUGHTER.
    His voice thundered / sometimes
    there was thunder in his voice
FATHER.
    "She's my wife / I love her /
    Never Gonna give her up /
    I love her!"
DAUGHTER.
    I grow up — my body
    can make a
    child
    I Do not but I can — make a child
    A child / a life / can come through me
    can come crashing through amniotic
    Fluid and Blood /
    It can come silently
    It can come thunderously
    My Grandfather / Long Dead
    Ghost dances in the hills /
    His wife / my Grandmother
    calls me — "Dark Girl
    Monkey Girl
    animal / Dark / Monkey
    Girl! / The

  elders don't want you /
  WE don't want you!" She says /
  my Grandmother says
  My cousins on my mother's side /
  My Black hand side says —
MOTHER.
  "You're Black / what's this
  Indian / no such thing as
  HALF-BLACK!"
DAUGHTER.
  They / my cousins / my Black hand
  mother side cousins say put
  down my Father's Tlingit walk / Ghost dance /
  put aside sweet guitar licks and
  the Red / Blues of my
  Grandfather / Put aside
  his slick / sleek
  Rock 'n' Roll res / Boston Bop /
  Put it Down /
  Shoot it on
  Down
  My Red hand / my Father's
  hand / His mother / my
  Grandmother / cousins
  Don't call my name
  I'm the "dark" / Monkey Girl /
  Don't have a name —
  An uncle / he calls my name /
  says my name /
  only him / my Father's Brother /
  my uncle / he says
FATHER.
  "Drop the
  Black Blood / walk like a
  Skin / Drop the Dark / Darkey
  walk / You're a SKIN"
DAUGHTER.
  How can I drop the

>   walk of Southern Black
>   Girls / the walk heated / hip
>   walk of Southern high-heeled Black
>   Girls
> MOTHER.
> > *(Repeating.)*
> > You're Black / no such thing as HALF-BLACK
> FATHER.
> > *(Repeating.)*
> > Walk like a Skin
> DAUGHTER.
> > I answer to the voices
> > I answer to the voices in
> > DarkTown /
> > I answer to the voices in
> > BlackTown / The Town where
> > Black people live
> > I answer to the voices My Grandmother's Tlingit voice
> > That whispers in my ear
> > I see / dance with my Grandfather /
> > We sing a Red man Blues
> > I am Tlingit / Lakota and Blues
> > I am an electric slider / Tlingit / Lakota Ghost
> > Dancer
> > I've got Red / Black hands
> > I answer to all the voices
> > I know that Blind Lemon Jefferson did the
> > Ghost dance with Robert Johnson
> > and Robert Johnson before
> > selling his soul to the
> > devil pulled out the
> > Mojo and gave it to my
> > Grandfather who kissed it
> > and passed it on to my Father who
> > passed it to me — I've got Red / Black hands
> > Don't tell me not to Ghost
> > dance on the Res
> > Call for my ancestors

       on the Res /
       whisper Tlingit secrets to my Grandmother / dance / Link
       Wray style
       Down at the Res /
       I will rock the Res
       I've got
FATHER.
       Red /
MOTHER.
       Black
DAUGHTER.
       hands
       Don't anybody expect me to
       Shoot it
       Shoot
       Shoot
       it
       on Down

End of Play

BEAUTY'S DAUGHTER

BEAUTY'S DAUGHTER premiered in New York City at the American Place Theatre (Wynn Handman, Artistic Director) on January 25, 1995. It was directed by Peter Askin.

BEAUTY'S DAUGHTER

DIANE

DIANE. I've always done the slide. Like you never, never show your heart! *(She smiles.)* I mean you can kiss and fuck, but your heart? Naw! A love thing? That's TV and records and books but there's always somebody looking for it, right? And I have seen some tough-assed broads go down on account of it but they say, man, that you haven't lived until you felt it. *(Pause.)* It's more than just they say a grind / groin thing and me? Well, me, I could never see me doin that — goin down like that.

That's what I thought but then right? I'm in a car and I see him — this man and he's 6' 3" with long black hair and blue eyes and a mouth like a girl's — a pretty girl mouth and he's the most beautiful man I've ever seen and as I watch him walk, I'm wondering how his voice sounds. I wanna hear how his voice sounds, what kind of sounds come from your sweet mouth? I wanna say *(She pauses.)* I hate feeling this way! *(She smiles.)* But I love it! *(Beat.)* I can't be a punk-assed bitch going soft over a love thing? What's that — love! *(She stops.)* It feels so nice. *(Beat.)*

This one night I'm across town and I'm in this bar and there's some woman on her last legs trying to pick up young boys and she's singing along to Van Morrison and she's slurring — a terminal blues right? And he walks in and she wants to talk to him, wants to hold him tight, but he's in his head and doesn't want her, and I say to the woman, "You can't do that. Can't suck someone's youth and try to make it your own." And she laughs and walks to another part of the bar and him — Cal — he looks at me and smiles and I'm excited, right? Fidgeting in my seat — like Elvis. See, when I'm mad or excited I begin to move — right leg, right hand move like half-anarchistic boogie, half-Elvis and I feel "the King". The King is reaching for me now, 'cause I'm excited, right?

Elvis is rippin through me now or is it Bessie Smith comin down in double time screaming a ball 'n' chain chant. And Cal sits next to me and he's got a Celtic / mystic eye and he says soft 'n' slow, "I'm from Dublin, you?" "Harlem," I say. And when he makes a point he touches my leg and cocks his head to the side and the vodka and beer is slidin down our throats and somebody called "Closing time" but I swear I didn't hear them, didn't want to hear them.

I walk the streets and I see him, could be two in the morning, could be two in the afternoon — it doesn't matter 'cause Harlem and Dublin are rolled up into one. *(Beat.)* We had dinner in my house and I read him some of my poetry —

I could have given birth at sixteen
But I was too busy dodging bullets
I was harnessed in rhythm
Muscles taut
Thighs bent
Blocking blows
Praying for kisses

And he calls me a powerhouse. I fuckin loved it — being called a powerhouse! 'Cause it's a boy thing, a ballsy dick thing, boy thing man and we just keep trading black / Celtic / rock 'n' roll dreams and happy dancin to spastic operas of our own design. James Brown. Sam the Sham. Catch us if you can! *(Sheepishly.)* I don't sound like a punk bitch! Shit! I really hate this. *(She smiles broadly.)* Bullshit, I love it.

Me and Cal walk Dublin's streets full of music and noise. There's no difference between Grafton Street and 125th Street and Lenox Avenue. It's a Mich / Nigger blues. People trying to hustle you the some way they do in Harlem. Chicks with babies trying to cop some change. *(She pauses.)* This kid comes up to me and said, "I need some fookin money. Yer rich, yer American, I'll take yours." *(She pauses and smiles slightly.)* I looked at him and said, "Now boy, if you try and I do mean try to take my money, as God is my witness, I'll snatch you out of your pants and disconnect you from your asshole." Powerhouse! *(She laughs.)*

We go to Francis Street to check on a friend who was on the dole. We drink Harlem / Black Guinness in Grogan's pub and one night we sleep together. Don't make love. Just sleep together and he rubs my stomach and between my breasts and I don't move because I can't go down like that. It wouldn't have been right like that had I done it — had I loved him that night. I just knew it'd be incomplete, going down like that. Cal looks at me and smiles and strokes my face. I run my hands through his hair. Touching, we're always touching. We're surrounded by people in pubs. When I make that decision — I say, "I love you." 'Cause I do. This one night the thought police invade his brain and he's had a lotta vodka and ale and he's slacked-jawed and talking loud, judging himself, judging others and he thinks everything becomes crystal clear though muddy Guinness. He talks about people he no longer wants in his life and how he wants to get rid of them or shoot them down to the ground and I say, "What about me?" And he looks through me, blue eyes glassy and says, "I don't love you. Don't even know you." And here comes the King, I can feel the King coming. He's ripping through me now. So I get up and walk out, walk cool — a cool take no shit Harlem walk through Dublin but there's something crashing inside me / crashing to the ground. I'm on the floor crying like a bitch, like the punk-ass bitch I swear I'd never be. He's got my back now. I'm doing the slide.

PAPO'S MOVE

So there's this little boy
& he's got merengue &
a little desperation in his
move & he bops &
drops to the side
both to be cool & to
avoid his Father's blows &
in his walk when he
dips to the Ground —
talking streettalk / walkin talkin Spanish,
this boy, Papo, man
Got
Salsa Shoes

Got Mambo Blues
& when he rises from his
bop, he dreams of things
like fine desks & open
spaces where voices don't echo
like in Housing Project bathroom
walls & there's gotta be
a place where ideas are
written on luxurious white sheets
of paper &
ain't it a bitch
when chuchifrito grease hits you
in the nose?
& Mommy got a black eye
& Mommy, she got a black eye again
& Latin boys wanna be Latin kings
& Latin boys wanna be
Spanish Kings
& When Latin boys don't get shot
they get lost
Goin Down
Goin Down the block
Goin Down the block
again

PAPO

Aged seventeen, Puerto Rican male from Lower East Side. He has come to Diane's house pleading with her to do his term paper which is due in two days.

PAPO. Yo Diane — how you doin sis? Yo, I know it's late, y'know but like yo, I needed to see you — know what I'm sayin. *(Beat, looks around.)* Boy, you got a dope house, man. Look it all this shit. Yo, Diane, look at this chair — this is fly! It's gotta be an antique, right? See, I know good quality when I see it! Also before I forget, you look exceptionally beautiful tonight. *(Beat.)* Oh shit, that's a picture of Rimbaud. *(Beat.)* See, I remember what he looks like from his picture on the *Illuminations* cover. "I alone have the key to this savage sideshow." See, I remember. *(Beat.)* Yo, Diane, like I know it's late y'know but like I gotta ask a favor Diane? I really feel bad y'know showin up at your house like this and it bein late and what not, but — *(His voice trails off. Beat. Suddenly.)* Diane, you wanna make some money? Yo, I know you said that when you weren't performin you worked in an art gallery, right? Man, that ain't no real money — so check this out okay? I got a proposition for you to think about, okay? I really. *(He takes a deep breath.)* Okay. I'll pay you ten dollars a page if you write my term paper for me. *(Slight pause.)* Don't say no yet! *(Beat.)* See, my paper, right? It's due in two days, sis! Two days man. I can't do the paper in two days. Porqué? Porqué it's just impossible! See, y'know I had to hustle four days this week right? 'Cause you know like the bills were comin in real fast right? And yo, Diane *(Crosses himself.)* I swear, my pop is drinkin all the time now, right? And that's where the money is right? 'Cause you know like the bills were comin in real fast right? And yo, Diane *(Crosses himself.)* I swear, my pop is drinkin all the time now, right? And that's where the money is goin and shit and — now Diane, think about it, it's not like I'm dealin blow or heroin. It's only weed right, and I know it ain't right but yo, I gotta look out for my moms and sisters — you gotta understand. I ain't tryin to cop a plea, but yo, I need money! *(Beat.)* Anyway, this paper, right? It's for English Lit College Prep Course and the teacher — yo, man she ain't no joke! Her name is Mrs. Marks — Mrs. Naomi Marks and she's real strict. *(Beat.)* Diane — I had told you about her. She's the one that helped me get into Bowling Green State College, remember? Check this out, the thing is, even though I'm technically accepted, I still gotta have a certain amount of credits, right and yo, I'm only three credits short sis, so c'mon now! *(Beat.)* It's not like I'm stupid — you read my stories! You know the story about what it's like growing up on Avenue D? You said it was good remember? *(Beat.)* Know what Mrs. Marks said? She said, "Papo, you have the potential to be a great novelist. You've got light, you got perception." I wouldn't make that shit up. That's what she said Diane and she sent my stories to the head of the English Department at Bowling Green College and he wrote back personally to say I was accepted. *(Slight pause.)* What? *(Sheepish.)* Well, I had three months to do the paper. *(Beat.)* Diane, check this out though. I keep tellin you that things are bad at home now — see you oughta know 'cause your mother drinks too, right? So I know you understand. Also, it's not like I smoke reefer all the time. I smoke maybe twice a week. And shit! Like I sell it, but yo, I'm about takin care of my moms and shit. Yo, I gotta make that money, yo. *(Beat.)* Maybe you don't understand 'cause you're a female. Man it's hard bein a guy — specially if you're Spanish or black 'cause y'know, it's a guy — specially if you're Spanish or black 'cause y'know, it's a double thing of sex and race. Know what I'm sayin. Oh shit! Okay, okay! Women got it rougher than men — I'm sorry Diane — I was wrong — Damn! Don't kill me! *(Beat.)* In fact that's what my paper is about. The effect of Black and Hispanic male writers on American Literature. I chose Pini Tomas and James Baldwin but I can't read two or three books in one day. *(Sheepish.)* I didn't get a chance to get my books yet. *(Beat.)* Man, see I was gonna get them but, like anytime I go to Barnes and Noble right? That there's this homo who works there, but he's nasty to me, right? I checked out his name and it's Allan. I call him Allan the Butthole. So right, like the last time I was in there, he was all snotty and shit. *(Beat.)* See, I had to do this book report on *Les Miserables* for Mrs. Marks right? And I went to ask him for the book but I fucked up the pronunciation and said *Lez Miserables*, right? So him, he's behind the cash register and this faggot, man don't even look at me, man, *(Imitates him.)* "First of all, it's pronounced *Les Miserables* and it's in the classical section but of course you wouldn't know that." *(He shifts, cocky.)* Now I had to be chill right? 'Cause yo, Diane I wanted to hit this three-dollar bitch homo and I told him, yo, anytime I walk in here you're scopin like I'm stealin somethin and I know it 'cause I'm Puerto Rican. Well understand this. I'm Puerto Rican, not a spic. Treat me like a Puerto Rican the same way I'll treat you like a gay man and not like a faggot. Then I walked out. Hells naw, I wasn't goin back for the books. *(Beat.)* See Diane, I let that motherfucker know I ain't no punk porqué yo soy Boricua. See what I'm saying? The double thing about being Puerto Rican and a guy. See, if you were there maybe he wouldn't have done that to you. *(Beat.)* Tell you what, the next time I have a term paper I have to do, yo, I'll bring you in there with me well in advance and you can check this homo out and if he says bullshit to me you tell the motherfucker off, that's dope right? Diane — mommy please, please you gotta write my paper for me. *(Beat.)* Listen I told you what Mrs. Marks said. Yo. You wouldn't want to ruin the potential of a future genius. *(Beat.)* See, I know you can write that shit and hook it up, so it'll be real dope. *(Beat.)* What you writin here — let me see. Check it out. *(Bends over as if reading something on her desk.)* "I touched the shoes of Mary Magdalene on Avenue D." Yo, Diane, that shit is fly — See, c'mon mommy, write my paper for me. See if you bring that kinda poetic justice, yo, my shit will be hooked up, and I promise, yo, not to do this shit again 'cause I know the only person I'm cheatin is myself. *(Beat.)* See, next time, I'll hook it up, so that I have saved enough loot and I can quit scramblin and just do my school work. 'Cause yo, I care about my future. *(Beat.)* See, let me tell you what I plan on doin — check this out, I'll attend college in about a year, a year and a half, no later. See after I graduate high school 'cause even though I wanna cut back on dealin, yo, I gotta be realistic, yo, I gotta scramble like twice a week 'cause like I said, my pops is buggin out on Barcardi all the time now! And also before I go away I gotta make sure he don't hit my moms and sisters no more. See I can't be selfish, y'know. *(Pause.)* Sometimes, right, like even though somethin may be wrong — Like I know dealing weed is wrong — Like you gotta realize that the money I make is helpin out, y'know? See Diane, sometimes you gotta do certain things 'cause you know eventually it may pay off and help someone in the long run, right? *(Beat.)* Like you doin my paper — yo, like that right? I mean how many times can I tell you, that although I fucked up — unintentionally — that my future is in your hands. Say what? I know you ain't callin me a punk. *(Pause.)* Diane, de qué? Lissen, Diane — I don't let nobody call me that. Know what I'm saying? Yo, I don't like that shit. *(Pause.)* I'm a punk 'cause I can't leave? That's my family. Yo, I can't turn my back on my family like that. *(Pause.)* Yo, no matter how bad they are, they're still my blood — you don't turn your back on your own, man. Yo, I'm not you. I can't do that! The last time he beat her, man, he kicked her like she was a dog. I grabbed that motherfucker and said, "Hit her again, and I'll ram my shank up your ass." Diane, man, I'm beggin you please, yo please. Yo, I'll never ask you to do this again. *(Crosses his heart.)* I swear to God! Diane, remember, what did you say to me? You said, "Papo you got to make your life better and ain't nobody gonna give you shit. If you don't create a life for yourself, on your own terms, your life is not gonna amount to anything." *(Pause.)* Huh? You're disappointed in me? Yo, you disappointed in me? Well, I'm pretty disappointed in you too! Like you and me supposed to be friends and yo, you give me back when I need you. How do you think that makes me feel? Well, dat's what I'm trying to do Diane. Mommy please. So what do you say? I fucked up? Lissen you know what? I'm leavin your house. Yo, I already know I can't be all that anyway — writing books? Yo, that's bullshit — I'm leavin okay? Sorry to bother you. Fuck it, I'm gone. *(He exits.)*

THIRTEEN 'N' BLEEDING

>I am thirteen 'n' Bleeding
>'n' there are blood stains in
>Panties
>And the Catholic school
>Uniform itches my skin and I'm
>Told that I gotta watch
>Myself now
>'Cause
>I'm a girl now and
>I gotta get my hair
>Pressed 'n' curled 'cause I'm
>A girl now
>And
>If I wanna go to Randall's
>Island to shoot dice and
>Play stickball with a gang
>Of boys, I can't

'Cause I'm a girl now
And
If I dream of
Touching boys differently it's
Because I'm becoming
A young woman now and
If I dream of lipstick
Traces, it's because
I'm becoming a young woman
Now ... but I think
"What about my leather jacket
And how I wanna wear it
With one earring, with the
Bold / cold air of a
Reinvented female."
And I'm Thirteen 'n' Bleeding
Bleeding — a girl / woman
Now with blood
Gushing from between
My legs, for the
Next forty years
And
The woman I'm supposed to
Emulate is standing
Before me caught up in
Some inebriated spent
Perception
And
I can't believe I sucked
Milk from those defeated
Breasts or
Whispered childhood secrets
In those withered ears and
I don't want to have babies
Give life from red — gore —
Blood.
I'm thirteen 'n' bleeding
In a Harlem living room

Left to flick switchblades
In the dark

BLIND LOUIE

Blind Louie. Heroin addict, aged mid to late fifties. He is junk sick and in need of a fix. He shines shoes for a living but today business is extremely slow. Louie is desperately waiting for Diane so he can go cop. Music comes up, something like Gil Scott-Heron's "The Bottle."*

BLIND LOUIE. *(Listening real close. He tries to steady himself.)* Oh, goddamn, goddamn! — *(He jumps as he listens to approaching footsteps.)* Who's this? Naw, naw, man. *(Beat. He begins to shuffle back and forth playfully as he senses Diane coming.)* Okay, I know it's you now! Yeah, the walk, man — that steel, slick walk, man that Cadillac walk. Oh, yeah! Oh, yeah! *(He stops.)*
    Hey, Diane or should I say Lady Di? How you doin baby? I know you fine. *(Rapidly.)* Yeah, babe, know how I can tell one person from another? By the walk, man, definitely by the walk, man. Y'know? Like the person that jus' pass me by jus' now, man — was a dude, y'know 'cause like his shoes scratched the ground. *(To the man.)* Hey man, pick up your feet! You walkin like you dancin a slow drag. Hey Diane, I hope that cat got much bank. He's hard on his shoes. With women, man, y'know women wear heels these days, click-edy click boom, click-edy click boom, know what I'm saying? That's music. *(Calls out.)* Now these two dudes who are walking up this way now they're wearing sneakers. *(He yells to them.)* Hey, my brothers! Dig this, one o' y'all is wearing Air Jordans — In fact, the brother on the right is wearing Air Jordans — 'cause you got a glide in your walk, man, 'cause them sneakers glide like a Cadillac, you dig. And my brother on the left, well you brother-man, I'm sorry, you got on Pro Keds. See, Pro Keds make a squishy sound man. *(Pause.)* Say what? How'd I know? Shit! You

---
* See Special Note on Songs and Recordings on copyright page.

be surprised what a blind man can see! Take care brothers! *(Beat.)*

(Sniffs the air.) Diane, what's that perfume you wearin — Wait! — Don't tell me! it's Wrappings by Clinique. See workin outside o' Macy's is all kinds of smells. Women wear perfume, men cologne. See, Aramis, now that shit got a real heavy smell. And like Escape is really for the summer. That damned Polo is for faggots. But Wrappings is all year round and it suits you Diane. It really does. *(Beat.)*

God, business is so bad today, Diane — you wouldn't believe it, y'know? *(He wipes his nose with the back of his hand. Beat.)* See, ain't nobody on the streets which means they ain't no walkin shoes, which mean ain't no shoes for me to shine which means they ain't no money. *(Beat.)* Remember how I useta have money, Diane? Man, I was sharp — sharp, man. *(Beat.)* When I played with Howlin' Wolf, dat's the most money I evah made, man. Did you know that? When I first started giggin. I was makin 'bout forty, fifty bucks a night then Wolf heard me play and he give me a big raise 'cause he said I played guitar like honey drippin from my fingers. And then I was makin two, three a night! Shit, I was boss, man! *(Beat.)* See, dat's when I bought that red Cadillac and you called it a "choo choo train." *(He sniffles.)* And I bought you a buncha dresses and toy trucks, 'member? Any time I came off the road giggin, man, I made sure, man, I gave money to Beauty for you. I'd always say, "Beauty, put this money in the bank for Diane." *(Beat.)* You always knew when I was comin, man, you jump outta bed like you wuz looking for my Caddie headlights, yellin, "Daddy two, Daddy two! Play something for me!" And man that thing got to me. Before I did anything man, didn't care how beat I was, man, my ass could be draggin, man, I didn't care 'cause my baby girl wanted to hear the blues. *(Shakes his head.)* Hot damn! My baby girl. You know you'll always be my baby, Diane. *(Beat.)* And you callin me "Daddy two, Daddy two" — Shucks, didn't bother me one bit. I understood it, man — 'cause although I made you, Arthur raised you. And Beauty would rather forget about me, man and I can dig that. *(Beat.)* Shit, I'd rather forget — about me too. Beauty told me it's 31 years today. Hot damn! Ain't that a bitch. I remember him sayin, "Louie now you got to look for Diane and Beauty 'cause I'm not gonna be around much longer." *(Beat.)* It's like he knew he was gonna die, y'know? Arthur was a good cat, a 9 to 5, stone cold, steady

Freddie, home at 6 cat. I couldn't do that Diane. I am what I am. Diane, I tried to look after you the best I could. You know that don'cha? *(Beat.)*

Yeah, I was always buying you stuff, all that money I made, man, y'know. I took care of everybody but here I am out here now y'know and ain't nobody givin me the time o' day. 'Cept you, baby and I know you don't want to be here but, I appreciate it, I really do.

Lissen I'm a be straight up with you, Diane, I need money, as much as you can spare — now — see, I'm puttin my shit out heah — 'cause I'm sick, man, real sick — I gotta go cop — I'm sorry to be like this but I can lie and say I need it for somethin else y'know, stand here, and try and cop a plea and perpetrate a fraud. I'm not doin that, Diane. I'm a junkie. It ain't about being shiftless. I need it. *(Pause.)* No you don't understand! I need it. *(Beat.)* You don't understand how hard it is for me! I was a musician! I played with some of the greatest blues cats in the world. I had it all, Diane, and then I git struck blind like this. I mean, what the fuck did I do to deserve this, man? Why the fuck did God punish me? I ain't never hurt nobody. *(Defensively.)* Yeah, so motherfuckin, right? Now I shoot dope. Don't tell me nothin about tryin to git help and all that shit 'cause it ain't gonna bring my sight back. *(Beat. He pauses as he hears Diane walking away.)* Don't you walk away from me Diane!

I'll be goddamned! You walking away from me? After all I did for you? Goddamn! Ain't that a bitch? Ain't that a motherfuckin bitch! *(Beat.)* I need money, Diane, can't you see I'm sick? *(Beat.)* Look at all the money I gave you! Man, each time and I do mean each time I came off the road, I always gave you somethin. *(Beat.)* Goddamn, I'm so sick. I'm about to shit myself! *(Beat.)* Don't think 'cause you moved downtown you better than anybody else, he'ah. You still from Harlem, no matter where you live. *(He stops suddenly, totally changing his attitude.)* Say what? Oh, in my pocket? *(He feels for it.)* Oh, shit! I'll be damned! You sure did. *(Beat.)* Lissen, baby, I don't mean to be hard but you see how raggedy my shit is now y'know and the thing is, Diane, people got to look out for each other. Specially you and me. I'm your Daddy two. *(Beat.)* Diane, come here, come here. God, I feel so bad doin this — but if you can come by once a week say, 'round this time and drop off what you can — I'd 'preciate it, okay? *(Beat.)* Hey, and the shoe shine is on me! Lissen, I know you gotta go. You keep writin that poetry, he'ah. *(As she walks off.)* Hey, one day I'm coming to one of your shows. *(Beat.)* Lissen, don't forget about next week, heah? I love you. *(He exits quickly.)*

POEM

The retarded girl that rang the bell in Mt. Morris Park every midnight was found murdered
on the hill that year — that year in '63 when cancer ransacked your guts but you tried to turn your back and pour a drink and light another Cuban cigar
and how many times did you grit your teeth when you watched your wife rub asses with
nameless men who got their kicks from aging party girls
Too jaded for even a B movie screen did you really think when I came crashing
through embryonic fluid and blood that it would put an end to her shake dance and you
never did live to see the stance I took
Like walking backwards from mirrors, afterbirth still entangled in my hands or the knife I
learned to wield through pent-up fingers
While learning dances like "Monkey" and later the "Fencewalk"
Sometimes crying for you — Hallmark / Father's Day card-like tears — those kind of tears
usually reserved for little white girls or nice-looking colored girls on a 1960s TV program
where parents called their daughters "dear"
I was way past that
learning to scrawl the names of future legends (gangsters and would-be gangsters and
whores) on the labels of old 45s (like you, they're no longer alive).
Where I was told that hustlers were really Tango dancers in Blackface.
Lately though, sometimes in a rock 'n' roll / jazz / blues haze while talking to somebody in
hip / hop / bop time

or maybe cutting loose yet another lover I've come to hate, I whisper your name
"Poppy / Daddy / Poppa."

MOTHER MARY'S CHAIR

The heat runs fluid thru Sylacauga, Alabama
Red clay dirt where Mother Mary played
Where Black girls swam in deep rivers oblivious to snakes
And climbed high trees that held many lynchings.
Little Mother Mary sang
Sang sad grown-up music by people like Mamie or Bessie Smith
And people would wonder where a child so young could get that stuff from.
When Little Mary's mother parted her legs and Mary bore her head
Her mother turned away and went to lay on the backs of men whose wives beg them to stay
But they were determined to lay with Mary's momma light skinned
Some say satin to the touch
Mary's daddy lived crosstown and hard
Knife scars rippled from his coal-black face
And he drove a Cadillac and listened to the Blues
And on his death bed he called Mary's name
And she stared straight ahead aged fifteen stoic 'n' proud giving no reply
She spoke about the whippings women get irate no good husbands
Who beat the gowns off their wedding wives
And would later laugh high 'n' proud 'n' she vowed it would never happen to her
In New York
Or maybe Oklahoma or Sylacauga
There'd be a man who'd hold her tight
Remove cloth from bone
Her virgin cries reaching far into the night
Or maybe it was God who layed Blessed hands

Beyond fragile cradle screams
Beyond muffled baby cries way into her fading arms

MARY ASKEW

MARY ASKEW. Y'know Bit, I played Jimmy Reed for Diane when she was five years old and you know what she did, she closed her eyes and rocked back and forth like she understood it. Really felt it, you know. *(Beat.)* That's what the blues is anyway — feelin. You got to feel things. *(Beat.)* Lord I wonder where she is, it's gettin so late. Lord, it feels good to get rid of this stuff, you know Bit I got a lot of stuff. Ain't it funny, Lord. Oh hell this dress here. This dress is the dress I made special for our first date, Bit. You remember? Lord, I went crazy goin through all them — Spiegal catalogues tryin to find this pattern. I was so happy I almost hit the ceiling. Diane's goin to like this — it should fit her nice. *(Picks up photos out of box.)* Oh Lord. Look here, oh Lord. Bit, here's a picture of Charlie in front of the Tip Top Club. Lord, my brother Charlie was smart. *(Looks at another photo.)* Oh my Bit, here's a picture of you and me in front of your mama's house. Oh Jesus, Diane's not going to believe this. Know what Diane said 'bout old pictures? She says it keeps folks alive. Like if you look at a picture a long time, you feel like you right with the person and that the people is talkin to you. *(She smiles.)* Lawd, that chile. But you know I don't feel no need to have it no more. All these things. All they are is things, you know. *(Beat — she pulls a sweater around her.)* Lord, it's gettin a little chilly. *(Beat.)* I can't wait to see the look on Diane's face when I give her these records. Lawd that chile may go through the roof. *(Picks up 78s one by one.)* Lawd, Ma Rainey's "Love Sick Blues." *(Picks up another.)* Oh my, Bessie Smith's "Sugar in My Bowl." *(Picks up another.)* Robert Johnson's *(Sings "Love in Vain.")* Hot damn! *(Another.)* Memphis Minnie's "Memphis Blues." That woman could play hard like a man.

One thing I really want to give her — oh God where is it? *(She rummages through a box.)* Oh, Jesus — here it is! *(She pulls out a necklace.)* Lord Bit, I remember the night you gimme dis and told me you loved me. How long ago was dat? *(She pauses as if to fig-*

ure.) Sixty years ago. *(She pulls on necklace.)*

I would wear this necklace and float down da street. Float and mens would alway' wanna talk to me, too. *(Beat.)* It seemed any time I wore it, I would jus'. I glow. Didn't matter what kinda dress I had on, honey, it could be the ugliest dress in the world — this necklace made me look like new money. Made me feel like — new money. *(Beat.)* I really want Diane to have it. *(Beat.)* Bit, when I tell her you gimme dis, she's gonna hit da ceiling. *(Beat.)* Lawd, dat girl is somethin, really somethin. Just as sweet as she can be.

Dat momma o' hers makes me sick. She said, "Dat necklace ain't worth nothin and neither are dem old-time records." *(Her face hardens.)* She jus' said dat to make me mad 'cause me and Diane are close and always have been close. *(Beat.)* Old drunken, pissy bitch — how Diane was born to her I'll never know. *(Beat.)* Diane told me and her she wanted to play blues guitar and y'know what her momma said? She said, "it ain't feminine!" Shit! I almost hit the ceiling! I said, "Diane, girl, you learn them blues, hear? Don't let nobody tell you a woman can't play. Girl, if you feel it you can play it. I gotta whole bunch a Memphis Minnie records that I'm gonna give you." Remember how we used to go see Memphis Minnie, Bit? *(She sits heavily.)*

I always feel ya 'round me, Bit. I always do. *(Beat.)* Da otha day when Diane called and she was talkin about fallin in love, you know with a little white boy but don't matter, love is love. Anyway, she was feelin kind of skittish and she said she wasn't goin to get involved with anybody no more. She said, "Mary I have tried — God! I have tried. I can't keep gettin up just to get knocked down again and again. Besides you Mary, I hate peoples — Peoples always want something from you. Wanna suck you dry. Mary, you — you're the only one — the only one I can hold on to, you're family." *(Beat.)* Man, Bit, that thing upset me so bad — 'cause y'know that's a horrible way to live. Y'know but God, I understand it — I really do, 'cause that goddamn Beauty *(Beat.)* — 'scuse me Lawd — did a job on that chile and Lawd knows that damned Louie useta could play the blues, but without a guitar wasn't worth a shit. And I told her, "Baby, give it a chance and if it don't work out you know one monkey didn't spoil no show. You can't cheat yourself out of love. You gotta keep feeling things to stay alive you know and you gotta find someone special to talk to 'cause y'know baby, I'm not gonna be here forever y'know." Then she asked me when I have a problem who do I talk to and I said, "Bit," and she said, "But he's dead, Mary," and I said, "Oh, no he ain't, baby, and not only do I talk to him, he answers me. And guess what else? We sometimes dance together." *(She plays a song like "I'm in the Mood" by John Lee Hooker.* Lights change as if Mary were a young girl. She dances as if Bit were dancing with her.)* You hold me close, Bit, and I feel my back straighten and I rub my hands down your back. Your strong back and I'm fifteen again wearing my flowery dress and necklace. My rosewater perfume mingles with your sweat and my head is on your shoulder, and we dance, we just dance. And they ain't no such thing as New York tenements or crowded up subways. It's you and me and blues music down South and it's warm, it's always warm down South. *(Beat. She goes back to being an old lady.)* Yeah, I can't wait to give this to Diane *(Looking at necklace.)* but I sure hope she comes soon. *(Beat.)* Y'know, Bit, when I tole Diane that I talks to you regla, she said, "Oh Mary, dead people don't talk," and I said, "Sure they do. Just 'cause you can't see somethin don't mean it ain't there. You can't be afraid to feel things." *(Beat. She goes to window.)* Lord, the temperature's droppin, it's gettin chilly. Hope she comes before it gets too dark.

SAL/SOUL

>I could have given birth at sixteen ... but I was too busy dodging bullets
>I was harnessed in rhythm
>Muscles taut
>Thighs bent
>Blocking blows
>Praying for kisses
>Watching from forbidden windows
>Black & latin boys who stayed
>High on Saturday nights &

---

* See Special Note on Songs and Recordings on copyright page.

Did "the Grind." Their
Auras crystallized in magenta
Heroin & freshly cut veins
With voices splattered on urine-
Stained walls, they rode
With Christlike posses against the
Bodies of unready young girls
Frightened little boys
Seasoned in penetration
Volatile little boys
Coming like the pulse of New Cities

ANTHONY

It's 5:30 P.M., and Anthony is semi-dressed up after work. He's in the Radio Bar and it's happy hour! He's a regular and he comes in every day after work. Music plays, something like Charlie Parker's "Billie's Bounce."* He enters yelling to various people in the bar.

ANTHONY. Hey Gerry, how ya doin! Hey Lorraine, ya lookin good, honey! *(To bartender.)* Hey Lenny, how's it goin babe? *(He rubs his hands.)* Awright Johnny Black — nectar of the Gods. *(He shudders slightly.)* I tell ya Len, today was shit, y'know? Yeah I know every day is shit but today was really shit. *(He sips from other shot.)* So fuckin busy and y'know I'm always ruinin my fuckin clothes. Everybody I know that works in the fish market, their clothes are always fucking ruined. *(Beat.)*

I just fuckin can't stand the thought of goin home right now! I just can't! *(Pause.)* Therese's gettin fatter and fatter and it ain't 'cause she's pregnant 'cause I don't touch the bitch! *(Pause.)* I'm cold for sayin that? Listen, Lenny, I like big women but not fat women and wife or not, the bitch is fat! *(Beat.)* Look Lenny, let me explain somethin to you. I'm thirty-one years old, right? I'm mar-

---
* See Special Note on Songs and Recordings on copyright page.

ried twelve years — twelve fuckin years! I'm trapped, right? I got two kids — ten and eleven years old. Lenny, I'm still a young man, and I'm fuckin trapped! *(Beat.)*

Tee Tee is the laziest bitch in the world. She don't clean the house right. She hasn't learned to cook and here she is twenty eight years old, lookin fifty! *(He leans forward.)*

Lenny, I work twelve-thirteen hours a day so she don't have to. There's no excuse why this bitch can't cook or keep herself in shape. *(Pause.)* The problem is I married too quick. When me and Tee Tee were kids together, we thought we were so much in love, right, and my cousin Jimmy says to me, "Anthony, listen, youse two are young. Don't get married so quick. Go out get laid, have a pisser." *(He smiles wryly.)* But of course I don't listen, right? so this is where I am today.

Lenny I met this girl right, y'know? and she's a black chick right? *(He shakes his head.)* A tough motherfucka! She was at my friend Mano's wedding. *(Pause.)* Yeah, right you remember him ... sure you do — he came in here with me a few times — Anthony Manacuso — we call him Mano because my name's Anthony too.

Anyway at the reception, right? Tee Tee's there and she and the — rest of the cuchinettes they're talking to Mano's wife Gail who's no prize. Lenny, I wouldn't fuck her with your dick. And a few guys I haven't seen in years from my old neighborhood in Red Hook — they're there too right? and to tell you the truth, I really don't wanna be there, but Mano's a friend, y'know?

So anyways — this black chick — Diane's her name, is sitting off to the side by herself. I look over at her and smile. 'Cause I never made it with a black chick before, right? And I always wanted to see if they were any better than white broads. Y'know a lotta white guys wanna do it. Y'know what they say? They say once you did black there ain't no going back. So anyway, she smiles back and I notice, y'know that she's big, but not fat. Big. In proportion. The way Tee Tee used to be. So I go over and say, "You know I think you're good-lookin and they need to get rid of words like nigger and guinea. Know why? 'Cause I wanna put my tongue in your mouth." So she gets mad and says, "Let me tell you one thing; the only reason why you came over here is because I'm the only black person at this wedding! Guess what? I don't have a problem with that but you do so do yourself a favor 'n' get out of my face before I hurt you!"

Now, I'm standing there fuckin slammed right? So I say to her, "Listen, I don't care how fuckin big you are. Woman or not, you hit me, you're dead!"

So, then she says, "First of all, my being a woman isn't the issue 'cause I'm more man than you'll ever be and more woman than you'll ever know. Second, I know I'm a big woman but you're still a man so technically I can't whip you, but I'll give you such a fight, you'd wish to God you stayed home today. In other words my name is Pain and I will inflict. Now do you really wanna fuck with me?" *(He pauses.)* So now, I'm quiet right? And I'm also scared out of my mind. Part of me wants to give her a smack, and another part is in love, right? Lenny! This chick is so tough! So check this out, I say, "Hey Diane, c'mere Rocky! — I'm sorry baby, I apologize. Come wit me to the bar to get a drink!"

So we go to the bar right? and I say, "Diane, let me order you a rum 'n' coke 'cause I know blacks and Ricans like that." So then she gets mad again and says, "Order me a Stol on the rocks, lime garrish and stop being an asshole." *(He smiles.)* So now I know I'm in love right? And we're hangin out at the bar and we're talking and stuff and the DJ starts playin Sinatra, Jerry Vale right? Of course every guinea wedding there's Sinatra and Jerry Vale and since all of us are in our thirties — the DJ started playin disco. I ask Diane if she'd like to dance and she says that she hates disco and likes rock, old blues and some jazz, and I say, "You like jazz?" *(He crosses himself.)* Lenny, for the next two hours, we're talking jazz. *(Beat.)*

    A woman is Jazz,
a tight, taut woman in a red dress,
or a sleek catlike woman
standing long and cool throwing
glances and she can stick you hard and long,
or short and sweet jazz
and you are dyin to hold her tight
and play her play her all night long,
fingers goin down her back and up her sides
and down again, jazz.
    The foxiest, sexiest fuck you will ever come across,

the kind of woman that will break your heart,
jazz pure fuckin jazz is,
that is what jazz is,
a woman,
a lady,
a bitch,
jazz.

(*Beat.*) All of a sudden I feel like cryin, right? I mean I'm talkin to her and fighting back tears (*Pause.*) See Lenny, jazz, it's so a part of me but I can't touch it anymore y'know? I can't touch it. (*Beat.*) Diane was really listening, y'know? Like the way I wished Tee Tee could listen which of course she can't. (*Beat.*) Diane's a poet and I never knew a poet before. Y'know I guess her being creative, she's gonna understand where I'm coming from, y'know? (*Beat.*) So now Diane is smilin now as we're talkin right? And she's warming up y'know? And she suggests that maybe y'know, I could pick up my horn again right? And that she could write lyrics and I excited right and God, Lenny, she's really beautiful, man. See Lenny, I never had a woman say to me, "Anthony, you got beauty in you so you must be talented." She said that, Lenny.

(*Beat.*) She also called me a pain in the ass. (*He laughs.*) But she said when I talked music, my face became beautiful. (*Beat.*) Jeezus, I sound like a queer right! (*Beat.*)

Y'know, Lenny, Diane's outta Harlem y'know and she grew up tough like we did but c'mon, you can't compare Red Hook with that fuckin place! (*Beat.*) Y'know, she just fuckin saved her money right? And left there 'cause she said she had to be a poet at any cost even if it meant leaving everybody behind. (*He shakes his head.*) Can you imagine? Just walkin off like that! That takes balls — like you Lenny — you leavin Brooklyn the way you did — shit! Fuckin balls man! (*Beat.*) She told me that I could pick up my horn and just do it. I said whaddaya mean? — just do it? and she said, "Anthony, if you're lookin for guarantees, there aren't any. But one thing I can guarantee is if you don't pursue your music, you will be miserable the rest of your life." (*Pause.*) I got so scared that I just wanted her to hold me, y'know Lenny 'cause this woman — if I was with this woman — nothin and I do mean nothin could hold me back. I mean other broads talk, y'know this one — she does — right? *(Beat.)* After a while I just kept thinkin, God, this woman is incredible. I kept saying that to myself over and over.

After a while, we went outside 'cause it's really hot and I'm dyin to ask for her phone number and like seconds later, Tee Tee walks out and yells, "Anthony, me and the kids are ready to go home now!" *(He shakes his head.)* Diane looks at me like I'm fucking crazy right? and Tee Tee's standing there lookin like a fuckin whale. So what can I do? Bada bing bada boom, I introduce them to each other, right? And Diane says, "Nice to meet ya. I'm outta here babe." I'm doing the slide. I take Tee Tee home. *(Beat.)* Lenny, that night I go down to the basement and for the first time in like five years, I pick up my sax. It feels so good just to hold it and finally I put it to my mouth man, and with each note I can taste feel Diane. That woman, that bitch. She's all over that fuckin horn and my dick's gettin hard and I close my eyes real tight and I'm up there with Miles / Parker / prez and Diane is just sittin there smilin, smilin, smilin. And Lenny man, I'm making love to this horn — fuckin this horn and then I hear, "Anthony, what's all that noise down there? I need my beauty sleep." My life hits me in the face. Dead in my fuckin face. *(Pause.)* I ain't goin nowhere. *(Beat. He pauses and smiles sadly.)* But I can always do a shot — of Johnny Black, right babe? *(Beat.)* Oh no, don't worry about me. I won't get drunk — I can't — I gotta work tomorrow. But — *(He inhales deeply.)* — I just can't take goin home right now, y'know? *(He exhales.)* I'll be okay. I'll go in a little while. *(Lights and music fade.)*

BEAUTY

Beauty — late fifties to early sixties. Alcoholic. Mother of Diane. Beauty is speaking loudly to annoy Diane as she hears her going up and down the stairs. She pours a drink and takes a sip. She reaches into a box. Pulls out a feather boa and dances around drunkenly as if doing a striptease. She suddenly stops, goes to the box and picks up a picture of Arthur.

BEAUTY. God! Look at this. See this? *(Loudly.)* This is valuable. This is a Van der Zee photograph. This is worth somethin not *(Loudly.)* them ole-timey records and bullshit and bummy dresses — damned bag lady dresses. What the fuck would somebody want with that shit. I can't believe somebody is crazy enough to climb them stairs all day to collect junk. Fuckin raggedy dresses and records made before I was born. Why the fuck would somebody break their ass to get that shit? See most children would be grateful to collect valuable things from their parents like photos and jewelry — real jewelry. *(Goes to box.)* God, Arthur's gold cufflinks — see this is worth money, real money. I guess I gave birth to an ingrateful child who's too ignorant to know what good quality is and bad quality is. *(Beat.)* Not to mention selfish! Thirty-one years ago today my husband, her father's gone and this chile can't even acknowledge me sitting here — no can't do that. *(Beat. Goes to the box and picks up a dress.)* This is a real dress. I bet if I get this appraised it's worth somethin. Hell, when I bought this dress thirty-somethin years ago, it cost over a hundred dollars. *(Holds dress against herself.)* When I wore this dress men went ape-shit! Honey, I knew I was together, jazzy! I was what they called BTP — Built To Please. See if it was me, I would be grateful for what was given to me. I would look at these things and think, "God, this is what family is about." I would thank God I had a mother who cared enough about me to save somethin of herself. *(Picks up a watch.)* Classy, classy things. *(Beat.)* Arthur always worked hard to take care of his family. I always appreciated what he did. *(Picks up photo.)* Look at how handsome he is here — God that man loved me. He loved his family. Thirty-one years ago today — God has he been gone that long? *(Beat.)* You got to admire a man like that who took you in as his own. If Arthur was alive right now, it would hurt him to know that his own child, his only child is not treatin her mother right. He'd be — appalled to know that his own daughter cares more about a dead tenant than her own mother. *(Beat.)* Why the fuck would that chile wanna go collect that cheap shit Mary left her — not to mention how much it's gonna cost me to fix that apartment up there. If she knew she was dyin', why didn't she get rid of that ole ratty furniture. *(Calls.)* Hey, Diane, if you're so sentimental about Mary's things why don't you take that stick-assed furniture outta here! *(Beat.)* You love Mary so much you probably would wanna take that cheap assed furniture, right? You loved her so much I guess you wish I was the one dead. Well, that's okay. You think what you want. At least I really tried to make somethin of my life. See you dropped out of college and you know what that makes you? A failure. How in the hell are you gonna write poetry or whatever? You gotta go to school to do that. *(Beat.)* Let me tell you somethin. As a black dancer I had to struggle.

I had to work stripping at private parties and before that I was in a traveling dance troupe, the Black Bottom Dancers, that was kind of risky … or may I say "risqué" … and everything. See, I couldn't work downtown high class places in my day not even in New York. Bitches like Gypsy Rose Lee and Ann Curio had that all sewn up. Not a black face in the crowd. *(Beat.)* I got over 'cause I was real light-skinned and could pass for white, but it was dangerous. If a black woman was darker than a paper bag — that's right, darker than a paper bag — and if they'd found out that I had one inch of nigger blood I'd gotten kicked dead in the ass and everything. Diane, you got it easy! I'm not one of those mothers who ran the street to have fun, honey. I didn't have to leave the house. Mummy's right here.

Well, here you are, thirty-five years old now and still fuckin — up. Talkin about I caused you a lot of damage! *(Sarcastic.)* Aren't we melodramatic? Can you imagine? My husband dies and I'm a widow woman who has to raise a child alone in the world and you're talkin about I caused you damage? You ruined me! I was in labor with you for 36 hours. You were 12 pounds and 5 ounces. Rough on you?

They had to give me a Caesarean. *(Shows scar.)* Feel it! I want you to know how they cut me. How they ruined my body. You stole from me. I was a dancer. I was pretty. My body was gorgeous! And you say I caused you damage? Hell! Bitch, you robbed me! *(Pause.)* That's right, I'm calling you a bitch. A fat bull dyke lookin bitch!

Problem is I spoiled you. You don't know how hard it is out there. You had it easy but when I die you'll see. That's right baby, when I'm gone you'll say, "Oh, I wish I treated her better." or "Oh, now I understand since I got a child now. Ma was right." But see, it'll be too damned late by then, see? So you want to bring up how "mean" I was. You know what I say to that? I say "Bull! I got mine!" I did right by you and I think you're crazy. One day you'll need me. You watch it ... one day ... and me? I'll be in my grave. It'll be too late.

RAT DREAMS DESCENT INTO HELL — 1994

The body of the rodent was
Smashed against my only
Dress and its eyes landed
On the bathroom wall and
My mother and neighbors
Were laughing at this
Permanent fixture — laughing
Next to the acid-stained
Faces of street fighting
Women hungering for the
Kisses of another
Woman's husband which was
Next to the burnt-out
Alley
Which was sealed off with
Auschwitz bobbed wire
Which at one time held
Rat-infested buildings
Which housed bitten children
Some who continue to
Stay 'n' play stickball
Emulating
The movieola
Innocence of suburban kids
Who drink chocolate malts
Leaving mustaches and
In continuation of this
Rat crawl Rasta men invades
My bed in a dream

Within a dream where
Balso Snell type nightmares
Parts my legs with the
Hush consent of the urban
Bushman
And 5:00 A.M. becomes
3:00 P.M. and spasms from
Not being able to
Put a knife thru my
Gut infuriates me and
I pick up the phone
Instead
And a Black girl's volunteer
Voice tries to keep me
Alive via Ma Bell
(She's new at this, I can tell)
And not equipped to deal
With suicide just yet.
Later with $15.00 saved
I go downtown to drink
Vodka to sleep (this is
Money saved
From my artist modeling
Job — my only job)
Where a boy/student
Calls me fat and apologizes
And
Sometimes I just wanna
Jump in the grave 'cause
I can't make the grade,
Coming out of the
Subway, a dead man
Fighting, permanent slumber
Dressed in raggedy
Clothes is drinking cheap wine
With
Determination and he
Stops dead in his tracks

And says to me, "Shit, girl!
You see how down 'n' out I am!
If I can smile and try 'n'
Live, why can't you"
I smile back Temporarily
Rejuvenated but as soon as I
Hit the street where I
Live, the stench of the
Crack pipe hits my nostrils
Smoked, by neighborhood
Boy / girl whores pretending to
Cum / Selling nothing for
Cheap
It dawns on me that the
Only thing that separates
Me from them are the books
In my room
And
When I sleep, I scream
Myself awake
And
When I sleep, I
Scream myself awake
And
When I sleep, I
Dream of my mother's
Birth planet Uranus
Thinking it must be a cold place filled
With the upturned noses
And elastic hands of
Strangulating bitches.

DIANE II

Diane is standing onstage with white spotlight speaking her thoughts aloud. Music opens, something like Suzanne Vega's "Bad Mystery."*

DIANE. It's 5:00 A.M. — I'm crying / crying in the fetal position like a punk-assed bitch I said I'll never be / and I hear "Love you? I don't even know you" And Mother Mary she's at the Pearly gates / I can't reach you at the Pearly gates / I'm not ready for that / the Pearly gates. And I need to talk to somebody 'cause I'm close to the bone / crashing. I find my friend Arlene. She's in her dyke bar / a 24-7 / a gin-soaked bar room keep on rockin dyke queen. Making Tanqueray plays for other girls who are dressed up for each other — but I don't care 'cause Arlene's my friend and how many times has she sat with me as I loco-motioned — about another love / lust thing. And I need to talk to her 'cause I'm feeling spent and everything is real close to the bone. And her / Arlene is asking me about wanting to kiss a girl. "Have you ever thought about girls, Diane?" she asks and me, I'm taken aback and I say "Yeah, I have fantasized, but I really believe the love between a man and a woman can be beautiful. I'll never get that / hold that so I'll just be solo and do the slide." And she's talking about men, not being able to handle me 'cause I'm too strong. "They're afraid of your strength 'cause they're punk-assed men / men can be so insensitive sometimes." As she slips her hand to my thigh as she's saying this / moving her hand up and down my thigh / saying this. And she's supposed to be my friend. I think she's trying to rape me. She's trying to rape me and I grab her hand and say, "you want me to fuck you, huh — that what you want? / Okay, bitch, I'll fuck you." I wanted to ram my fist in / hurt her / draw blood / draw the blood of this sincere rapist.

Suddenly I'm in bed with my mother, I'm thirteen years old

---

* See Special Note on Songs and Recordings on copyright page.

and still made to sleep with her, her body is a mass flabby, blubbery mess and she reeks of Scotch. She wants me to hold her and she speaks in a baby voice. A fucking baby voice about how much she misses my father and how lonely she is and how she wishes her mother was alive and how she sometimes thinks of suicide. Suddenly, tits are on top of my chest, she wants me to hug her. I refuse. She punches and kicks me and rolls over. Eventually, I hear her snoring. I get up and get a large pair of scissors from the kitchen and return to the bedroom. I raise the scissors above her but I can't do it. I can't kill her. Like I can't rape Arlene. I put on my jacket and break out. *(Pause.)* I haven't seen Arlene for months and it's understood that we can never hang again. *(She walks to center stage. Something like "King of the New York Sheets" plays and dies out.*)*

People can't be trusted. *(Beat.)* Only Mary, Mary's the only one. The rest of the human race is a mess of parasites. This fucking collective mass of parasites who use guilt to put each other down, use each other and call it love when all it is is desperation. Because they're afraid of being alone. All that shit is bogus. *(Pause.)* So I don't want it at all man.

> You know, I've walked this walk before where razor cut glances can slice the skin of the toughest whore. I've heard this rap before.
>
> Like when you get your first kiss and hear music and the music is gonna swell and get bigger 'n' bigger like an Italian movie. I've witnessed this scene before like when someone's mother chain smokes while they drink and they talk about when they were young — 'cause when they were young they were good lookin and men dug them, and they take a final pull on their drink and the smoke comes out their nostrils and they end the whole rap by saying "My God, ain't life a bitch."
>
> I dreamt this somewhere. I touched these shoes of Mary Magdalene on Avenue D. Blood was flowing

* See Special Note on Songs and Recordings on copyright page.

from her feet. Spanish dances were hanging on shiny, aluminum gutted tenements echo another dark black Nigger future (Phantasmoryonia, they called it) Somebody's popping chewing gum or maybe it's the click of the hooker's shoes pacing the pavement three o'clock in the morning.

Lovers are tongue-kissing in the doorway and the souls of young boys are trapped underneath the hoods of stolen cars and love is something cranked up real loud on a dilapidated stereo for everybody in the street to hear. Or, maybe love's a rumble or maybe it's Neptune putting on black velvet gloves and dancing again.

DIANE (TO PAPO)

Diane goes to the FDR Projects to speak with Papo to reassure him that she's still friends with him. They are sitting on the benches talking. Her morning was spent moving Mary's things from the Harlem house to her apartment downtown. Her mood is melancholic but hopeful. Music comes up, something like Lou Reed's "Romeo and Juliet."*

DIANE. *(She shifts, uncomfortable.)* Papo, know what? I'm not gonna cut loose 'cause I wanna see you dance, a Rumbaud / James Baldwin / Piri Thomas dance
a Spanish stroll
Literary merengue
Wanna see you reach inside yourself and write it down on sheets
  of paper
beyond the housing project back staircase wall
through your bowels through your groin and I'll be there
I swear I'll be there

* See Special Note on Songs and Recordings on copyright page.

I promise not to cut you loose
I can't cut you loose ... hermano, baila, hermano.
(She smiles. Beat.) Today in Harlem, I was collecting things
things from a dead friend
meant to keep me alive and precious, sweet things. Like music and pictures
pictures of dead people screaming that still continue to talk — live — live. And I slapped five with the ever-changing, expanding man who was proud to share his secrets and I don't wanna see you trading stories on Avenue D with defeated men, too old to rock and roll
too young to die
determined to keep the ditty in their bop at any cost
talkin about what I could have
should have been as the temperature drops and the only thing left to warm your heart with
is a swig from a bottle
I know 'cause I've done my time screamin Mommy / Mama / Daddy / Pappa
Why did you leave me through cracked Harlem plastered walls while Mommy lays limp in
a Johnny Walker Black / Teachers Scotch haze at peace in her velvet prison and Daddy
croons the Boneyard Blues forever and coldly.
But I'm gonna keep Mother Mary's precious things
her precious, sweet things and I'm gonna spread them at your feet, Papo, 'cause I wanna
see you dance, wanna see you dance.
But you can't give me fly boy excuses about glitter and gold while rolling your eyes
skyward looking for a sign to justify a bogus plea 'cause I can tell the difference in your eyes
I can tell when they're in a Panama red mist or shielding your father's Bacardi / Boriqua
blows or when you've tranquilized yourself, thinking the future becomes clear in a nickel
bag and why you can't stand in one place 'cause you're dodging the gun and I'm not gonna

let you go down like that
go crashing down to the ground like that
I wanna see you take a stance
I'm gonna make you dance.
(She shifts a little.) Y'know, Papo, the temperature's droppin. It's gettin chilly. But I'm
right here, bro, I'm right here. I promise you, I won't do the slide.

End of Play

PROPERTY LIST

Box with photos and necklace (MARY)
Stack of 78s (MARY)
Drink (ANTHONY)
Drink (BEAUTY)
Box with feather boa, photo, gold cufflinks, dress, watch (BEAUTY)

MONSTER

MONSTER was originally produced in New York City by the New York Theatre Workshop in 1996. It was directed by Peter Askin.

MONSTER

THERESA. Marsha — remember the voices / the paper-thin Harlem wall dwellers / in / around this house / raging / screaming voices / bitter beat / angry / voices / around this house / this house Grandmother Sophia owned / then later my mother Beula / who just died / just died / can't believe / she just died / gone / left me this house / this bitter / beat house / and I can still hear the voices / Nana Sophia raging / snarling / voice — "beat, beat, beat your children" / more voices / my mother Beula's voice / make sure that men want you / be pretty for the men / act pretty for the men / for the men / then the voices from the tenants / hanging on to every word / they listen / listen to me dream / talking to myself / she's crazy they say / listening to that ole weird shit / who she talking to / they're listening to me / laughing at me / they would you know / they would / you knew / felt it / how it could suck / suck / suck / you / me dry / and those voices off the avenue / the voices in Harlem / 122nd Street and Madison Avenue, Harlem / cut / you / me / cut / you / me / cut me down / down to the ground / those voices / that went through you / straight to me / words / voices meant to cut / you / me / down — hey, here comes the white girl / actin like a white girl / Walter, Tootie, Brother and Peaches would say / aiming their voices through you / at me / aiming their voices at me / watching me / standing on the corner / watching me / standing on the corner / smoking reefer / wasting time / they had nothing but time / their voices crashing into this house / Marsha, I want to break down their voices / Marsha / smash their voices / I would, you know / but there's Emma / Emma's voice / face / smile / how can I sell the house / leave Emma's voice / smile / love / behind / I need to go / sell the house and go / painful here Marsha / it's painful / I can't hear mine / my own voice / I got a hole in my heart / I can back it up / I can / I want / need to burn down their voices / 'cause it's my time / My time.

SOPHIA. Now Theresa, listen well. I know you still a child. A lot of what I'm saying may not make sense to you, but remember, Nana is leaving the house to your mama for now, but after your mama dies this house will go to you. Do you understand? This is your house. You hear that Beula? It is written in my will that this child will be the sole heir of this house. Not those nappy-head niggers you mess around with. So Theresa, you listen to me. You are not to live like a nigger, do you understand? You educate yourself by reading. By listening to the white people talk. By staying in school, you hear? You are to marry a light-skinned man. House, money, everything in your name. If you have a child, especially a girl child, you pass on what I'm sayin, even if you have to beat, beat, beat it in to her. Don't do what your mama did, Theresa. Look at her as an example of what not to do. You listen to me. You listen to Nana, 'cause I wouldn't tell you nothing to hurt you. I tried to teach your mama not to live like a nigger. What happens? She marries the darkest, crustiest, no-account one she can find. I'm sorry to have to tell you that, Theresa, but it's true. Your father didn't play a role in your life at all. He was ill-equipped. Inferior. You see honey, dark-skinned men are evil, ignorant! Your great-grandmother, my mama, Christine, died at forty-three years old. You know why? Because she married a dark man. The man that fathered me. Notice I didn't call him Father, I just said fathered me. He hated me for being the lightest of us kids. Hated me. And he would beat, beat, beat me like the nigger savage he was till I bled. It broke my Mama. Broke her. But it made me strong. After she died that man stayed in the bottle. Stayed in the bottle. And on his deathbed he said, "Oh Sophie, I sorry. Please Sophie, I want you to be my baby," in that horrible geechy accent. I just looked at him and said "You Bled my mama. I loved her. *(Beat.)* I don't love you, but I will provide for you. If you love me as you say, you sign house, land, everything over to me." And Theresa he did. Everything. 'Cause he was dyin. He was scared. Weak. And I took. I deserved to take. I tried to tell your mother this, but she ended up a drunk just like him. Theresa, I look at you and thank God you were not born dark. Look at you, a yellow girl. A bright yellow girl. You know, Nana use to be bright too, bright, like the sun. But with this lung cancer I've grown dark. Dark. All my life I've tried to take care of myself, and look what happens to Nana. Get struck down with lung cancer. Never smoked a day in my life. All on account of your mother smokin. Yeah, your mother smokin, drinkin herself to death, and determined to take everybody with her. You, me, everybody. Right Beula? You satisfied? You did this to me. You want me dead. Well you gettin your wish. Theresa, your grandfather and I gave your mother everything. When we lived in Bonneau, South Carolina, at the height of the Depression we took care, Theresa. We took care with money. When we came to New York, still in the Depression, we lived well. We were the only coloreds on the block that owned property. Owned. How many colored people can say that? All I asked your mother to do was appreciate what was given. Theresa, you listen to Nana. Listen. Because of this cancer, Nana does not have long on this Earth. Use your lightness to the best of your advantage. Read. Read books. Don't sit in front of a television. Read. Nana only had a third-grade education, but I always read, and I'd listen. You know how Nana learned to talk properly? By listening to the white people talk, and you must listen too. I see you do well in school, your grades are good, you're smart. You can go far Theresa. You must go far. Now I'm goin back to South Carolina 'cause I can't function like I used to. Otherwise I'd take you with me. God knows I can't keep watchin your mother destroyin herself. But you remember everything I said, you hear? You remember. Now if you don't listen, if you drop out of school, marry something pitch-black, when I die if there's a way for me to come back and haunt you, I will. As God is my witness, I will. Do you hear me Beula? That goes for you too. I'll get you. I'll haunt you.

THERESA. I'm walking 122nd Street and Madison Avenue trying to walk erect and correct, trying not to get lost, trying to block out my grandmother's and mother's machete voices screaming through at each other. I'm seeking quiet or hard-core riffs from a sparse guitar / Walter, Tootie and Brother are dancing a Kool 'n' the Gang / mandrill dance and Tootie and I / Tootie and I / I look in Tootie's eyes / a second / her / my eyes lock / a second / I / she / we remember a conversation about a book we both read three years ago / we connected three years ago / on my stoop / two black girls on a Harlem stoop / then somebody / her brother they say /

does her / does her they say / and she cries / goes hard / street hard / doesn't call my name no more / in a second / I / she / we / remembered just now / I knew / felt / saw / she remembered / let's go back to three years ago / she turns her back / keeps on dancing / they / they don't want to let me pass / but I keep my hand on my shank / If you're on 122nd Street and Madison Avenue trying to find your own, and you know it's not there / where a game of hopscotch means dodging used syringes / you learn to cut / you better learn to cut someone deep / On 122nd Street and Madison Avenue in my room / my head / my headroom / I discover Iggy, Lou Reed, Hendrix, and I wanna James Baldwin, Kerouac, Jean Genet, John Cocteau, Go, Rimbaud, Go, Rimbaud. I better find the longest shank I can. What I listen to, it bleeds out to the streets. I get called "white girl" and Mother Beula shakes her head / wishes me dead / I brace myself for that long walk from 122nd Street to the subway contemplating ways to kill everyone / kill myself / chanting a genocide / suicide mantra. I walk downtown / Kerouac / Baldwin / they said it's downtown, East Village / black, yellow, white, brown / jazz / jazz / more jazz / people / me / I'm lookin for rock 'n' roll / I'm lookin for home / lookin for family / and the people are wearing different kinds of clothes / and the people are walking a walk / different / the same / of / everybody else / I wanna get next to / in / connect / how do I do that / get into / next / connect / be a part of / want to know their names / cafe / bar / rock 'n' roll people / what are your names? / and another black girl / sister / rocker gives me the power sign as we hear the New York Dolls from a car radio / and I think it might be / may be / down here / East Village / might be / may be / alright

alright

alright

But I'm only fifteen, and soon I gotta go home. Soon I got to put my hand back on my shank. Soon I gotta prep myself for that subway / bus ride that takes me back to Harlem and Lee, Brother, Walter, Peaches, Tootie they're still on the comer 'cause they got nothing but time "White Girl," "Here comes the white girl" they yell 'cause they say, they figure if you're black / you shouldn't read / they figure I'm black / kick back / stay back / back in the ghetto / where you belong / they say that / they say not to read / or hear /

see colors / see / hear / music / different kinds of music / to wanna live elsewhere / somewhere / somehow / good well 'n' fine / it means to be white / not black 'n' proud / black 'n' proud / in the ghetto / stay black in the ghetto / stay black 'n' poor / in the ghetto where you once / always / belong / cut / shoot / gun 'n' shank they say means to be black / stay black / stay black / cut / shoot / cut / don't dream of leaving / 'cause you're black / and Kool 'n' the Gang is at full volume screamin out "Hollywood Swingin" / Kool 'n' the Gang / is just loin groin riff / Harlem ghetto riff / a loin groin fuck-in-the-alley ghetto riff / I've seen / heard that / all the time / all my life / against the wall / against the wall / but Jimmy, Iggy 'n' Lou gonna give me more than that / I walk to the house / ease the key in the door / peep down the hall / Marsha, my homegirl, looks out / shakes her head / her mother and my mother are Scotch high / Scotch high / Johnny Walker Red high again.

BEULA. Oh there goes Mommy's baby! C'mere Theresa. Look Scotty, dere's Mommy's baby comin in. Wait, wait, don't go to your room so quick. Come give Mummy a kiss. No? You don' wan' give Mummy kiss? Well that's alright. Mummy loves you. You may not love Mummy, but Mummy loves you. Look Scotty, you see how pretty my baby is? Oh what you mean don't call you baby? As long as I live, you'll always be Mummy's baby, right Scotty? Look at her. You see her? See she's grown tall, right? She'll probably be tall like my Mama Sophie, but too bad she don't like to dress. *(Beat.)* Theresa, how come you don't like to dress up? Me and your grandmother always dressed. Always. Even Marsha wears a dress once a week. And Marsha ain't pretty. All that psoriasis and stuff. I mean you pretty. And you don't take care. I mean Marsha, she actually looks nasty. But even she tries to take care with her appearance. Scotty, you tell Theresa, tell her that men like feminine girls, right don't they? They like girls to dress up … You would think that I don't buy her clothes or nothin, her dressin the way she does, right? All in black like that. *(To Theresa.)* Theresa, you fifteen years old dressin like some black bull dyke in mourning. No, no wait a minute. Don't go to your room when I'm talkin to you. I'm just tellin you for your own good. Now I'm glad you're smart and all, *(To Scotty.)* oh God, Scottie. She's smart. But she's runnin down there.

EMMA. Theresa! Theresa! Theresa, wake up baby! Heard you

callin my name way up in my house! I'm here darlin. *(Theresa signals that Beula's asleep.)* Beula still sleepin? Good. Yeah, she breathin easy now, ain't it. Lawd. Lawd, her face just as smooth now. Like she ain't got a worry in the world. Yeah, when the Lawd take her she won't feel a ting. Nothin. *(She looks at her.)* She don't look sick at all, do she? I'm cookin some okra soup for ya. I know ya like it and it's good for ya too. Yeah, ya got to eat Theresa. Take care of yourself. I see you beginnin to drink some, ain't it? You better mind. Don't fall inta dat. You should know better. *(She points.)* You see ya mama layin there. You seen what it done to her, right? It hard seeing Beula like this. Really is. Your Mama was a good woman. Just got lost along the way. *(Beat.)*

When your mama and me were girls together in Bonneau she was always nice to me. Always. Always spoke. Then when I come up here to New York and run into your Mama on 68th Street, she helped me get my apartment here you know. The lady I work for say she ain't want no sleep-ins, and that same day I seen your mama on the street and she took me to Ms. Sophie and said, "Mama, Emma need a place to stay, and you gonna give her one." An Ms. Sophie look at your Mama, and me, and finally say okay. So Theresa, your Mama got good in her. It's just a shame she couldn't stand up for herself. See, your Mama could dance. Lord that woman could move. She had come across a woman who had a dance troupe, and the woman come here to talk to Ms. Sophie about Beula joinin. And Ms. Sophie scared the woman, said, "My daughter ain't gonna stand up there shaking her tail for money and goin around the country like a damn gypsy. Dat's a whore's job." Theresa, that crushed Beula, really crush her.

That's why I believe your Mama started to drink heavy, 'cause everything had to be Ms. Sophie way. Like the way she run this house. How if anybody made a noise she bang the pipe. And how you could eat off the floor 'cause it was so clean. Man, I use to feel funny comin in here 'cause, like if I sat down, I feel I would dirty it up in some kind of way. And when Beula took it over things change. I bet Ms. Sophie turnin in her grave. I tried to get your mama to paint the house a different color. I never did like brown, it make things look sad. I like white and dark orange, they're warm colors like down South. And now, baby, it looks like this house is goin to you. You gonna own this house and I see you weighed down. I see how weighed down you feel, especially with Beula like this. *(Beat.)*

When you was a little girl I used to love to hear you read your stories, and poetry, and sing. Listenin to all kinds of music, an dreamin. Don't feel funny baby, I used to do that too. Talkin to myself and pretending I was a queen livin in a castle. I would tell my mama one day I was gonna live in a castle and she would point to the outhouse an say, "Oh yeah, dere's your castle right there." Everybody would laugh, but I ain' care. *(Beat.)* Theresa, you still a young woman, you can do something about them dreams, baby. I see you gettin hard, bitter. I know it ain't easy seein Beula like this, knowing she ain't got long. But because Beula ain't got long, you gonna have to make some decisions for yourself.

(Beat.) Sell this house an go, an live where you want. And don't go worryin 'bout me neither. I old. I done live my life and I can always go back to Bonneau, you hear? This is a death place. Now if you wanna live in Harlem, fine. If not, fine. Not all black people supposed to live in the same place. Don't pay people mind when they say that. Treat yourself good baby, or you'll end up like your mama there. Please. Yeah, Beula's still breathing good. I glad. Ya, let me go on an check up on that soup, and you think about what I said. Don't let them dreams die.
HERMAN. Theresa, Theresa. Theresa! Please, can you lower the music. I was trying to read and it's just so loud. I never understand why you play music so loud. I mean, how can you appreciate it? Assuming you call that music. Listen, now that I'm down here, I have a letter from a company saying that they're coming to appraise and need to see my apartment. So, Theresa — uh — I don't know, really, what to make of this, you know — these people coming here, you know, everything in chaos, you know, I mean, Beula dying three weeks ago, and now what is this, Theresa. If you're going to sell the building, I think maybe you should think about it some more. I mean, to own property is a good thing. *(Beat.)* Miss Sophie always said that — property is good, remember? That people — responsible people hold on to property and Miss Sophie should know, right? I mean, she took good care of this house and she always said to me, "Herman, Theresa's my legacy —

I know she'll do better than Beula. She's the true heir to this house." Yeah, that's what Miss Sophie said, that you'd hold onto the house. As for Beula, she was weak, but Miss Sophie always spoke highly of you. *(Beat.)* I miss her terribly. She was a good friend. She took good care of me. She was a good woman. You know, Miss Sophie would at least offer me a glass of water. Can I sit? *(Beat.)* You know, when I first came to America, in 1944, from Warsaw, the first place I came to was Harlem. The only thing I had were the clothes on my back and the only family I had left was my sister Nella. Harlem. It was great. Music, families — it was lively. The colored people have always been good to me, and Miss Sophie was one of the first people I met. She would come to my newsstand and buy three papers a day, and we would talk about segregation, the Holocaust. Me and Miss Sophie, we know hardship. She was so kind. *(Beat.)* I was living in a room on 119th Street but couldn't afford anything lavish. Miss Sophie didn't care. She said, "Herman, here is an apartment. It's yours." See, people who suffer look out for one another. Me and Miss Sophie know about hardship. Nobody ever gave us anything, and if they did, we would appreciate it, and care about other people. Yeah, Miss Sophie was one of the smartest people I knew. She read, read all the time. Me, too. That's how we became friends. You know how on Sundays I would have dinner and afterward me and Miss Sophie would come here and talk. Talk about books, everything from Kafka to Langston Hughes, and me, I thought I knew everything about everything, until Ms. Sophie fed me the chitterlings. See, I didn't know what it is so I say, "Ms. Sophie what is dis," and she says "Herman, you don't want to know," and I say "Yes, Ms. Sophie you tell me," and she says "Hermnan, chitterlings is hog guts." And I say, "What do you mean, 'hog guts?'" and she say, "Hog guts, Herman," I say "Vat, you mean like a pig?" and she said "Yes, Herman" and I say "You're feeding me pig guts?"and she said "Herman, pure pig." I vent up stairs, I trew up three times, I came back downstairs and had some more. You know why? It's all in the mind, all in the mind.

And me and Miss Sophie laughed and laughed. We were close, you know that. Like family — you remember. Remember how me and Miss Sophie would doublecheck your homework? Remember

Yeats? Huh? "Had I the heaven's embroidered cloths / enwrapped with gold and silver light / the blue and the dim and the dark cloths / Of night — light, half-light — I would spread the cloths under your feet / but I, being poor, have only my dreams; / I've spread my dreams under your feet; Tread softly, for you tread on my dreams."

I gave you a book of his poetry, remember? I gave it to you — that and Anne Frank. Before Miss Sophie went back to the South, she said, "Make sure Theresa reads, Herman, make sure." I did, remember? I saw to it that you read. Remember how I would come to make sure Beula gave you something to eat? And sometimes when she was yelling too much, how I would sometimes try to talk to her about the drinking? You remember those things, right? And yet you treat me like this, like I'm not human? You don't even come to me to say you're selling the building — or trying to sell it — like a decent person? Miss Sophie would — even Beula would tell me. How can you do this to me? Look how long we know each other. You know I have no place to go. You don't care what happens to me, is that it? I bet Miss Sophie and Beula turning in their graves. *(Beat.)* Theresa, listen to me. I have no money, nothing. Where can I go, huh? Where? Tell these people you changed your mind. You're not selling. You can't. You can't do this. The problem is, you're still dreaming as if you're a child. You're playing loud music like some damn teenager and acting like a child. This dreaming, this dreaming. You're being selfish. What you think, you sell the building, you find Utopia? You know the Nazis were dreamers too! When the people come and look at the apartment, Theresa? I won't let them in. Do you hear me? You'll have to break down the door. I won't let them in.

WINFRED. I'm thinkin of my girl, Theresa. An I'm feelin bad 'cause, you know, she ain't with me, right? I mean, you know what I'm talkin about? Like when your woman ain't around man. Dat's some hard shit. *(Beat.)* She write poetry and listen to classical and rock. You know 'bout that shit, right? Well, my girl, she like it too. *(Beat.)* You should see her man, she got soft smooth skin. Yeah, an she got much booty — I likes dat booty, man. In order for me to peep a broad she got ta have some ass. Gots to. *(Beat.)* Man, ever since we wuz kids she wuz writin poetry and stuff to me, through the wall. Readin through da wall. See, the buildin I lived in, right, her mother owned. Me, my sister Marsha and my mother live there. And me, Theresa an Marsha wuz friends. Tight, like family, right? Like I would look after dem, you know, 'cause it's rough. *(Beat.)* Like, I protect Theresa. Niggas round the way hated her 'cause she listened to rock and all that shit, and dressed different from them. But see, dey ain't know her like I did. Niggas wanted to get next to her, man — see, dat's what it wuz. An they wuz jealous, specially when I tole 'em how she would talk to me through the wall. *(Beat.)* See me and "Tee," see das what I call her, Tee right? We close. We have our own thing. Y'all wouldn't understand it. It was like a made-up language, the way she talks to me, an me listenin. *(Beat.)* "I spread my dreams under your feet. Tread softly, for you tread on my dreams." And she got this white gown on? And she ain't wearin nothin underneath it or nothin. And she got her hair, right, she got nice long hair and it's spread all over the pillow. And she sayin all this, lyin on the bed. And her legs is open. She's touchin herself. Puttin her fingers up there and gettin wet. She gettin real wet. And this classical music is playin, and her eyes is close, and I hear her call my name in our language. She's talkin through the wall 'cause she want me to come to her. But she scared 'cause she never did it before. *(Beat.)* So this one night I'm goin upstairs, but I sees Theresa's door is open, and I walks down da hall an she cold sleep in da bed. Like she waitin for me? An I walks over to the bed an sits down, an she wakes up an I say "Hey baby" and she say "Winfred, whachoo doin here?" an I say "Well you want me here. I'm here." *(Beat.)* Den she say, "Winfred, I don' wantchoo here, go!" And I'm lookin at her like she crazy an I say "Well, you tole me so, readin an talkin to me through the wall." Then she like, "I never tole you nothin. Get outta my room. Get the fuck out now." And then I gets mad 'cause all this time the bitch was playin me. Bitch wuz playin me. So I slaps the bitch an say, "Put yo' face in dat pillow, bitch, and don't even look at me." And she's breathin hard and she got on pajamas and got a big ass, nice big ass. Always did like dat big ass o' hers. I tell her, "I want me some of dat fat ass of yours, I'm gonna get some." And I'm lookin all dese posters of white boys 'cept for dat nigga Jimi Hendrix. An I goes over to him and pulls his face down, 'cause he ain't nothin but a white nigger too. And I say to her, "You a white bitch. You a real white bitch. Dat's why nobody like you." And I gits on top of her and she says, "I hope nobody raped Marsha. I hope nobody did to her what you doin to me now. I hope your dick rots, faggot." An I slaps her ass an say, "Bitch, you talks white too, huh? You talks like a whitey. Git bad wit me again." Then I slaps her across the head but she don't cry and I say, "Oh, you a hard rock bitch? You hard." An I pulls down her pajama pants and she says, "Oh my God." And I, "He ain't gonna help you now." And this white music is playing in the background and I'm sweatin and I know if somebody catches me I'm gonna go to jail, but I don't care. So I goes to the record player and takes that white rock shit off 'cause I can't get hard to that shit and put on some Marvin Gaye and my dick is on the bone. And I says, "You gotta nigga dick in yo' ass now, bitch." And she starts to cry and I say, "You like it bitch. Like it? I ain't no white boy in yo' ass. You got a man's dick in yo' ass. A real nigga dick, bitch. A black, black dick. Ain't no pink or some high yella nigga he'ah either. You ain't so high an mighty now, bitch." And I rides this bitch. I ride her hard and say, "You gonna 'member me, bitch. Yeah, you an all this white shit. I'm too low for you to talk to, huh bitch? Yeah, I got me a white bitch wid a nigga ass in Harlem." *(He closes his eyes.)* I'm ridin her, man I'm in her, man. She's my girl, my girl, an I say, "Theresa, let's make a baby." I say, "I want you to have my baby. An I'm a be the man of da house." And she cries real hard and says "no." And I slap her 'cross da back and ride her harder. *(He smiles.)* And she's sayin, "Winfred, why? Why?" She got her head in da pillow. An I tell her, "See you like it, right? You do." Then I gets off. Walks 'round da room. TV's too big for me to take. Then I goes back to da dresserette, dere's only five dollars, I takes dat and I say, "I got to go now, honey. But I'm gonna takin dis five dollars off da dresserette, okay." Then I piss all over dat white linoleum floor.

THERESA. *(A song like Patti Smith's "Gloria" plays in the background.*)* And Winfred's dick is in my ass. In my ass. He mocks me for liking rock 'n' roll. He doesn't like rock 'n' roll. Doesn't wanna rock 'n' roll. "White bitch," he calls me. And Patti's in the background chanting, "G-L-O-R-I-A," and I'm thinking, how could this happen? I'm blindfolded — cold, sharp metal and he

---

* See Special Note on Songs and Recordings on copyright page.

wants to make a baby, he says, "you and me," he says, and he could be the man of the house, he says. 'Cause he was always the man of the house, and I'm thinking, "I'm only fifteen. I don't want a baby," I'm thinking how God doesn't like me. God doesn't know I'm here. Or if he did, he doesn't care. I left the door open, how could I have done that, his dick is way in my ass. Winfred he's forcing his dick in through me. I'm going to shit myself I can't won't cry out. Winfred wants to know if there's any more pussy for the taking. My mother she's in her room. Can't / won't let him do it. Get next to her. "Put your shit on me," I say. "Get your shit off on me," I say. He's laughing, calls me a freaky bitch, freaky white freaky nigga bitch he says. Winfred he's forcing his dick in, through me and I say "I hope it rots motherfucker, I hope it rots." He slaps me. I talk to myself. I talk to myself. Maintain myself. Try to maintain some cool by talking to myself. 'Cause that's all I've got right now. Myself. Cold metal. Cold metal. In, through me. He mocks me for liking rock 'n' roll. He's in out of my ass. He's in out of my ass. Where is God right now? Where is God? Why God? There is no God. Take me now God. Take me now. He gets off, pees on the linoleum, kisses me, kisses me like a sister, like a child, says it's our secret. I'm blindfolded. I fall off the bed, belly crawl, belly crawl, through in his urine, my face wet with his urine it lands on my tongue, I'm belly crawling, belly crawling, I belly crawl to Beula's door she screams how she wants to die, she wants to die. "He should have killed us both," she screams. I'm on the floor doing a belly crawl, I can't feel myself, Emma she holds me close, Mommy Beula swigs from Scotch, she reaches for Johnny Walker Red Label, I reach for Emma, don't let me go Emma, please don't let me go. There are policeman, questions, and a hospital room. How'd I get here, I'm on a table, my legs are bound in stirrups. Stirred up legs. A male doctor Jamaican demands, yells, screams that I "open my legs, stop being foolish" he says, I unbind my legs, punch him, punch him, he screams like a punk, like a faggot hearted punk-ass bastard, then a nurse, a white nurse, pink lips uneven pink lips on pasty skin gonna try and jump and stop me, jump and stop me. I twist her arm back. I'll take you down bitch, low down bitch down. Down. I bring her down, down, down to her knees. Security guards come, warn me "someone will give you a hypo" they say, "be cool" they say, "better be cool" they say. I adjust myself, check, rearrange myself I become cool.

CHRISTINE. *(Hearing Sophia getting whipped.)* Oh Lawd, Lawd please let this man stop. Please, Jesus, let him stop. *(Beat.)* Eugene! Eugene! You stop beatin my baby. You stop. You stop it, hear? *(Beat.)* Oh Sophie. Sophie, please don' be angry. Ya daddy does get mad 'cause he don't understand you. He think you be tryin to sass him, but I'm a talk to him, hear? This time I'm a talk to him. I mean it. *(Beat.)* See, baby, your daddy had a hard life. People don' treat dark-skinned people right. White and colored. Can't you see dat? See how my mama does treat your daddy? And see, his own daddy was white and don' want him. See? So dat's why you daddy is the way he is. *(Beat.)* I does always tell ya daddy I love him. He figga 'cause I light I gonna rejec him one day. Know what he say? He always say, "Christine, one day you ga lef me for a high yella man." And I always tell him I ain'ga do dat. No I ain't gonna never. *(Beat.)* Sophie, you da lightest of all da chillin and you da smartest, so you try an understand ya daddy, hear? Try a understand him. *(Beat.)* You know, sometimes ya daddy does look at me hard, and sometimes I hate myself for bein light, hear? I hate myself. *(Beat.)* Sophie, you have to except certain things the way they is. You know, sometime you sound kind a uppity. Like them crackers. You can't be like them Sophie. Colored people can' live like white people. Why can' you 'cept that? *(Beat.)* Don' ask ya daddy a whole lot of questions, okay? And that way he won't beat ya, ya hear? *(Beat.)* See it would be different if Eugene was light like you an me. Da's why he mad, see? *(Beat — the beating sounds stop — Sophie enters.)* Sophie, don' look at me like that. Baby, please don'. It finish. All finish. You be alright. Don' think about it no more. *(Beat.)* Come on. Come on, sing me a song, Sophie. I ain't heard ya sing for long time. Come on, sing "One Day At A Time" with Mama. *(She sings — beat.)* No? You don' feel like singin? Okay. Den tell Mama about da book I seen you readin. Tell me 'bout da book, Sophie. Please. *(Beat.)* Sophie, please talk to me, baby. C'mon talk — talk to me, please. You don' hardly talk no mo. Ain't you got a voice? Where your voice at, Sophie? *(Beat.)* You can talk. Why you so quiet? *(Beat.)* Oh Lord, Sophie! Look at you, so fill up wit hate. Lawd God, you so fill up wit hate. Sophie please, let me hear your voice.

THERESA. Marsha, I'm watching a drunk street bitch / Ballantine Ale Triple X in one hand / holding it / caressing it / it's her lover / she's clutching it / clinging to it / her other hand slaps / a child / boy — / "little motherfucker" she says / calls him / "A no good motherfucker just like your father" / she says / and he has no voice / the tears / roll down his face / but / he doesn't make a sound / I'm listening to her voice / slurry all over the place / voice / hating her / hating this bitch / and me / I go outside / wanna kill / stop / her / I got the heart to / got the heart / I say / stop hitting that child / you stop / be cool / cool yourself / she turns /eyes / jaw / loose / gone / says / she'll "kill me" / "stomp my ass" she say's / and my blood it rises / rises to my head / expands to my fists / I'm on her / punching / stomping this / bitch / there's a crowd pointing / yelling / laughing / I feel good so good / Her blood lands on my shirt / on me / I'm mad / Marsha / mad / Satanic / glad / I'm killing / her / killing her / somewhere / her son screams / somewhere / I don't care / don't care / somebody / they part the crowd / somebody / puts their hands on my shoulder / I knock it away / I'll take you down / I'll bring you down / It's Emma / "stop chile" she says / and she's holding the boy / the crying boy with no voice / and / his eyes wide / afraid / I'm no better / than a animal / no better / not human / the crowd it disperses / and I'm walking / anger / in through my walk / his eyes / the boy's / they disappear / I'm animal / pure animal / I don't care about anything / anyone / dog eat dog / that's all there is / and Herman stops me / says something about his sister dying / Nella / her name is / was / and him / he's dreaming / dreaming Holocaust dreams / can't figure out why / I say we all gotta deal / cut their throat / before they cut yours / go for yours / His eyes fall / they fall / I walk on / I keep walking on / I move fast / thinking about fighting / thinking about fighting / killing / about how I beat the woman / with the little boy with no voice / and big eyes / I know why / Oh! God / I know why / I recognized myself / I beat her / 'cause I can see me / beating the boy / I saw myself slapping / the boy / the boy with the huge eyes / and / no voice / she is / me / the woman / the bitch / she is / me hitting the boy / I saw / Emma saw / I saw myself / and I knew I was no longer human / in that moment / no longer human.

Marsha / I've lost my way, Marsha / lost my way / how can I

get back / how can I get back to thinking, caring about the young boys and young girls like us who didn't / don't fit how do I get back to wanting to care about the meaning behind the words / music / I remember thinking are there people like us I use' to ask oh! Marsha, back then I use' to wonder "Do kids like us exist? Are they thinking of us now? Are they? Do they lie on their beds with closed eyes / hearing / dreaming where's music do they see colors do they hear outside voices pouring into their rooms / trying to shoot them down?" / I've often wondered how the rope felt around your neck / choking / bruising your neck / how painful / how strong were the voices that day / why was it worse than any other day / me I've often said why you? not me / why you? / I had wanted to do it to but didn't know how didn't know how to leave this house / all of it behind / but then maybe when you did it you saw / did you see / did you save yourself / part of you / did you save yourself? / or did you just go crashing down / down to the ground / letting them devour you piece by piece / and afterward they sat back / full lazy fat cat happy / Marsha / I really want to tell you Marsha / that I thought you were a beautiful beautiful black black dark black girl / but I was trying to keep myself for myself / I was only 15 / we were only 15 / but there is no difference between being 15 and now / I was / am busy trying to be cool / I was / am busy trying to maintain my cool / 'cause there are no answers for me in / against the altars of churches / I've got to find my way back now I've got to I can't do it your way I can't / it's my time Marsha, my time / I have to sell the house and go / sell, burn this house / burn down the voices / It's time to go / It's my time.

End of Play

NEW PLAYS

★ **AUGUST: OSAGE COUNTY by Tracy Letts.** WINNER OF THE 2008 PULITZER PRIZE AND TONY AWARD. When the large Weston family reunites after Dad disappears, their Oklahoma homestead explodes in a maelstrom of repressed truths and unsettling secrets. "Fiercely funny and bitingly sad." –*NY Times.* "Ferociously entertaining." –*Variety.* "A hugely ambitious, highly combustible saga." –*NY Daily News.* [6M, 7W] ISBN: 978-0-8222-2300-9

★ **RUINED by Lynn Nottage.** WINNER OF THE 2009 PULITZER PRIZE. Set in a small mining town in Democratic Republic of Congo, RUINED is a haunting, probing work about the resilience of the human spirit during times of war. "A full-immersion drama of shocking complexity and moral ambiguity." –*Variety.* "Sincere, passionate, courageous." –*Chicago Tribune.* [8M, 4W] ISBN: 978-0-8222-2390-0

★ **GOD OF CARNAGE by Yasmina Reza, translated by Christopher Hampton.** WINNER OF THE 2009 TONY AWARD. A playground altercation between boys brings together their Brooklyn parents, leaving the couples in tatters as the rum flows and tensions explode. "Satisfyingly primitive entertainment." –*NY Times.* "Elegant, acerbic, entertainingly fueled on pure bile." –*Variety.* [2M, 2W] ISBN: 978-0-8222-2399-3

★ **THE SEAFARER by Conor McPherson.** Sharky has returned to Dublin to look after his irascible, aging brother. Old drinking buddies Ivan and Nicky are holed up at the house too, hoping to play some cards. But with the arrival of a stranger from the distant past, the stakes are raised ever higher. "Dark and enthralling Christmas fable." –*NY Times.* "A timeless classic." –*Hollywood Reporter.* [5M] ISBN: 978-0-8222-2284-2

★ **THE NEW CENTURY by Paul Rudnick.** When the playwright is Paul Rudnick, expectations are geared for a play both hilarious and smart, and this provocative and outrageous comedy is no exception. "The one-liners fly like rockets." –*NY Times.* "The funniest playwright around." –*Journal News.* [2M, 3W] ISBN: 978-0-8222-2315-3

★ **SHIPWRECKED! AN ENTERTAINMENT—THE AMAZING ADVENTURES OF LOUIS DE ROUGEMONT (AS TOLD BY HIMSELF) by Donald Margulies.** The amazing story of bravery, survival and celebrity that left nineteenth-century England spellbound. Dare to be whisked away. "A deft, literate narrative." –*LA Times.* "Springs to life like a theatrical pop-up book." –*NY Times.* [2M, 1W] ISBN: 978-0-8222-2341-2

DRAMATISTS PLAY SERVICE, INC.
440 Park Avenue South, New York, NY 10016 212-683-8960 Fax 212-213-1539
postmaster@dramatists.com www.dramatists.com